ARTBOOKS

FROM CRESCENT MOON
PUBLISHING

Leonardo da Vinci
by James Pearson

Early Netherlandish Painting
by Rosalind Mutter

Memling
By W.H.J. & J.C. Weale

Van Eyck
By J. Cyril M. Weale

Piero della Francesca
by Naomi Haskell

Giovanni Bellini
by Julia Davis

Eric Gill: Nuptials of God
by Anthony Hoyland

*Minimal Art and Artists In the
1960s and After*
by Laura Garrard

*Vincent van Gogh: Visionary
Landscapes*
by Stuart Morris

*Mark Rothko: The Art of
Transcendence*
by Julia Davis

Jasper Johns
by L.M. Poole

Brice Marden
by Laura Garrard

*Frank Stella: American Abstract
Artist*
by James Pearson

*Maurice Sendak and the Art of
Children's Book Illustration*
by L.M. Poole

*Sex in Art: Pornography and
Pleasure in Painting and
Sculpture*
by Cassidy Hughes

The Art of Andy Goldsworthy
by William Malpas

*Andy Goldsworthy: Touching
Nature*
by William Malpas

Andy Goldsworthy In Close-Up
by William Malpas

Andy Goldsworthy In America
by William Malpas

Andy Goldsworthy: Pocket Guide
by William Malpas

The Art of Richard Long
by William Malpas

Richard Long: Pocket Guide
by William Malpas

*Constantin Brancusi: Sculpting the
Essence of Things*
by James Pearson

*Alison Wilding: The Embrace of
Sculpture*
by Susan Quinnell

Erotic Art In the 19th Century
By Cassidy Hughes

Erotic Art In the Renaissance
By Cassidy Hughes

Erotic Art
By Cassidy Hughes

The Erotic Object: Sexuality in Sculpture From Prehistory to the Present Day
by Susan Quinnell

Land Art: A Complete Guide
by William Malpas

Land Art In Close-Up
by William Malpas

Land Art In Great Britain
by William Malpas

Land Art In the U.S.A.
by William Malpas

Installation Art In Close-Up
by William Malpas

Colorfield Painting
by Laura Garrard

Bellini
By James Mason

Botticelli
By Henry Binns

Renaissance In Italy: The Fine Arts
By John Addington Symonds

The Life of Michelangelo Buonarroti
By John Addington Symonds

Michelangelo Buonarroti
By Charles Holroyd

Michelangelo
By Estelle Hurll

Michelangelo
By Romain Rolland

Correggio
By Estelle M. Hurll

Tintoretto
By S.L. Bensusan

Titian: A Collection of Fifteen Pictures
By Estelle M. Hurll

The Earlier Work of Titian
By Claude Phillips

The Later Work of Titian
By Claude Phillips

The Earlier and Later Work of Titian
By Claude Phillips

Bernardino Luini
By James Mason

Perugino
By Selwyn Brinton

Perugino
By George Williamson

Raphael
By Estelle M. Hurll

Raphael
By Paul Konody

Dante Gabriel Rossetti
By Esther Wood

Recollections of Dante Gabriel Rossetti
By T. Hall Caine

Burne-Jones
By A. Lys Baldry

The Whistler Book
By Sadakichi Hartmann

PRE-RAPHAELITISM

PRE-RAPHAELITISM

TWO LECTURES

JOHN RUSKIN

CRESCENT MOON

First published 1866. This edition © 2021. Reprint 2023.

Set in Book Antiqua 10 on 14pt.
Designed by Radiance Graphics.

British Library Cataloguing in Publication data

ISBN-13 9781861718259
ISBN-13 9781861718938

CRESCENT MOON PUBLISHING
P.O. Box 1312, Maidstone, Kent, ME14 5XU
Great Britain, www.crmoon.com

CONTENTS

NOTE ON THE TEXT

The text is from *The Complete Works of John Ruskin*, published by Smith, Elder and Co., 1866.

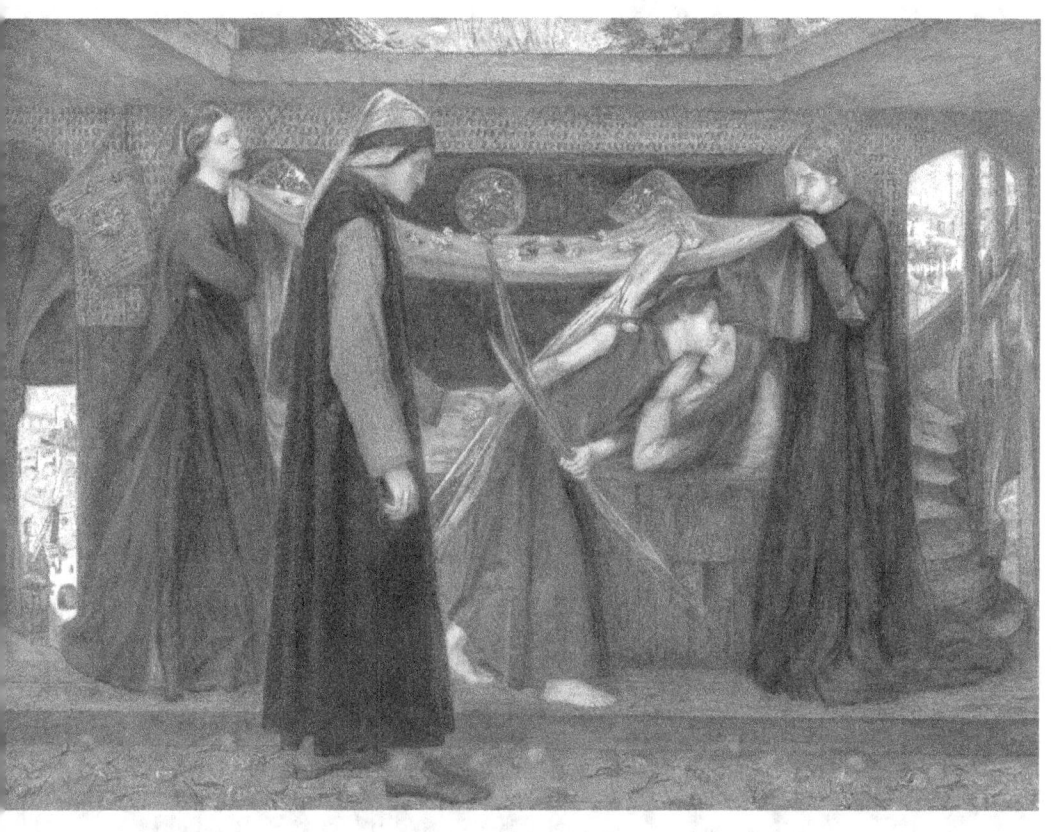

Dante Gabriel Rossetti, Dante's Dream, 1856, watercolour version, Tate Britain

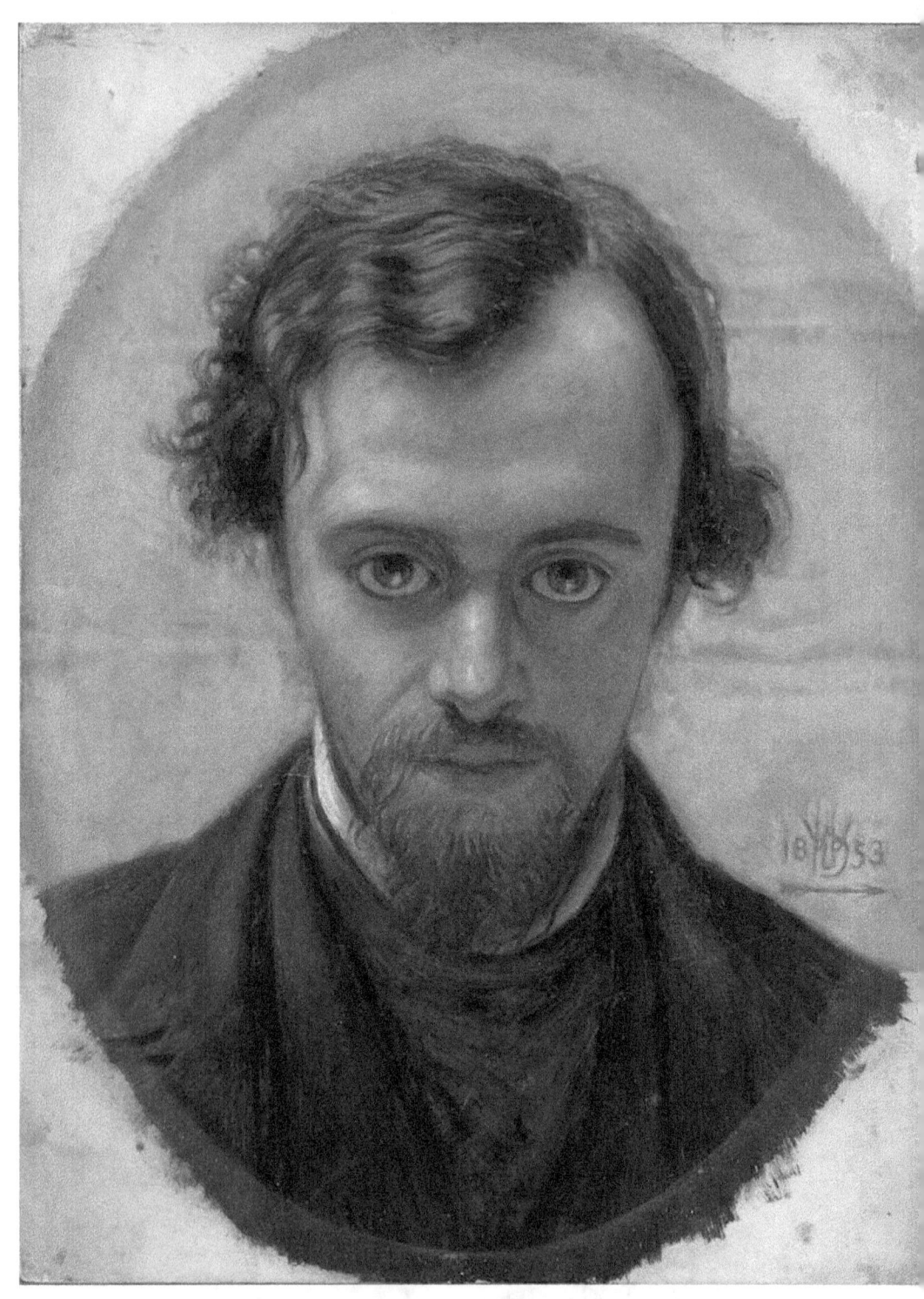

Holman Hunt, Dante Gabriel Rossetti, 1882-83, Birmingham

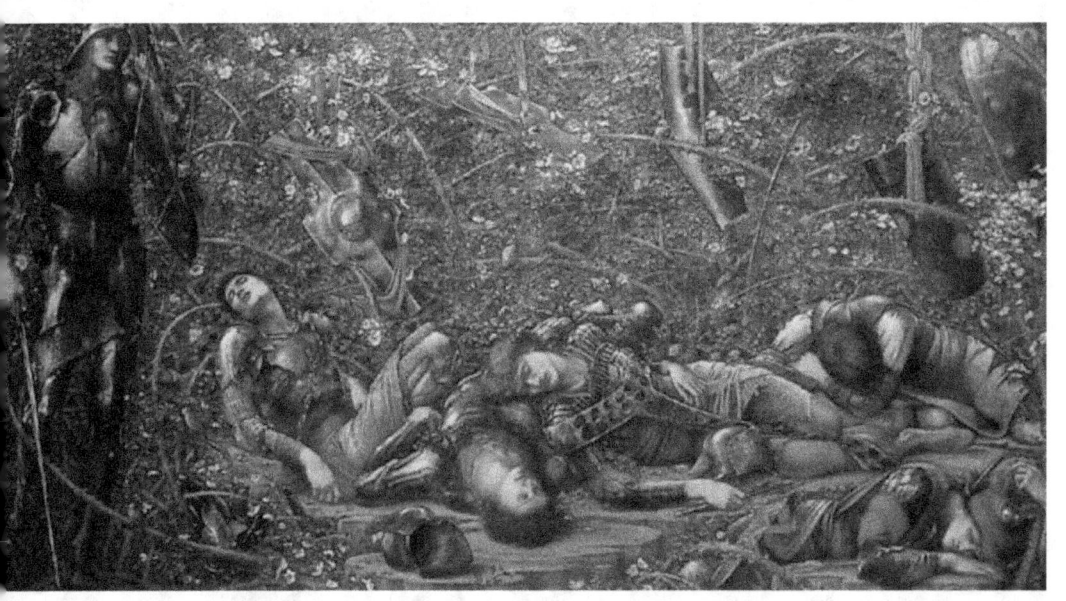

Edward Burne-Jones, Briar Wood, Buscot Park

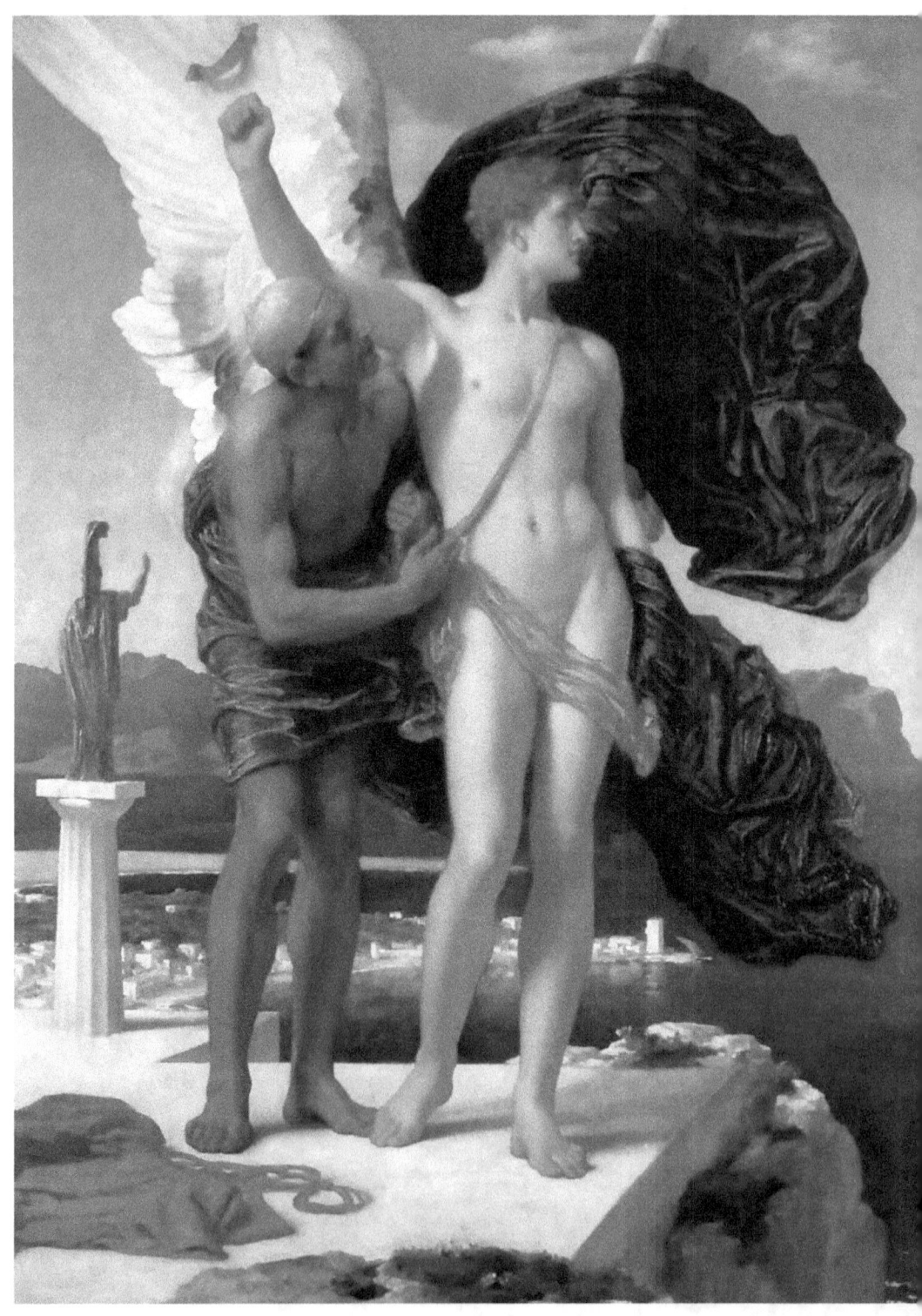

Lord Leighton, Icarus and Daedalus, 1869, private collection

PRE-RAPHAELITISM

1851

To
FRANCIS HAWKSWORTH FAWKES, ESQ
OF FARNLEY

THESE PAGES
WHICH OWE THEIR PRESENT FORM TO ADVANTAGES
GRANTED
BY HIS KINDNESS
ARE AFFECTIONATELY INSCRIBED
BY HIS OBLIGED FRIEND
JOHN RUSKIN

PREFACE

Eight years ago, in the close of the first volume of "Modern Painters," I ventured to give the following advice to the young artists of England: –

"They should go to nature in all singleness of heart, and walk with her laboriously and trustingly, having no other thought but how best to penetrate her meaning; rejecting nothing, selecting nothing, and scorning nothing." Advice which, whether bad or good, involved infinite labor and humiliation in the following it; and was therefore, for the most part, rejected.

It has, however, at last been carried out, to the very letter, by a group of men who, for their reward, have been assailed with the most scurrilous abuse which I ever recollect seeing issue from the public press. I have, therefore, thought it due to them to contradict the directly false statements which have been made respecting their works; and to point out the kind of merit which, however deficient in some respects, those works possess beyond the possibility of dispute.

Denmark Hill,
Aug. 1851.

It may be proved, with much certainty, that God intends no man to live in this world without working: but it seems to me no less evident that He intends every man to be happy in his work. It is written, "in the sweat of thy brow," but it was never written, "in the breaking of thine heart," thou shalt eat bread; and I find that, as on the one hand, infinite misery is caused by idle people, who both fail in doing what was appointed for them to do, and set in motion various springs of mischief in matters in which they should have had no concern, so on the other hand, no small misery is caused by over-worked and unhappy people, in the dark views which they necessarily take up themselves, and force upon others, of work itself. Were it not so, I believe the fact of their being unhappy is in itself a violation of divine law, and a sign of some kind of folly or sin in their way of life. Now in order that people may be happy in their work, these three things are needed: They must be fit for it: They must not do too much of it: and they must have a sense of success in it - not a doubtful sense, such as needs some testimony of other people for its confirmation, but a sure sense, or rather knowledge, that so much work has been done well, and fruitfully done, whatever the world may say or think about it. So that in order that a man may be happy, it is necessary that he should not only be capable of his work, but a good judge of his work.

The first thing then that he has to do, if unhappily his parents or masters have not done it for him, is to find out what he is fit for. In which inquiry a man may be very safely guided by his likings, if he be not also guided by his pride.

People usually reason in some such fashion as this: "I don't seem quite fit for a head-manager in the firm of - - & Co., therefore, in all probability, I am fit to be Chancellor of the Exchequer." Whereas, they ought rather to reason thus: "I don't seem quite fit to be head-manager in the firm of - - & Co., but I daresay I might do something in a small green-grocery business; I used to be a good judge of peas;" that is to say, always trying lower instead of trying higher, until they find bottom: once well set on the ground, a man may build up by degrees, safely, instead of disturbing every one in his neighborhood by perpetual catastrophes. But this kind of humility is rendered especially difficult in these days, by the contumely thrown on men in humble employments. The very removal of the massy bars which once separated one class of society from another, has rendered it tenfold more shameful in foolish people's, i. e. in most people's eyes, to remain in the lower grades of it, than ever it was before. When a man born of an artisan was looked upon as an entirely different species of animal from a man born of a noble, it made him no more uncomfortable or ashamed to remain that different species of animal, than it makes a horse ashamed to remain a horse, and not to become a giraffe. But now that a man may make money, and rise in the world, and associate himself, unreproached, with people once far above him, not only is the natural discontentedness of humanity developed to an unheard-of extent, whatever a man's position, but it becomes a veritable shame to him to remain in the state he was born in, and everybody thinks it his *duty* to try to be a "gentleman." Persons who have any influence in the management of public institutions for charitable education know how common this feeling has become. Hardly a day passes but they receive letters from mothers who want all their six or eight sons to go to college, and make the grand tour in the long vacation, and who think there is something wrong in the foundations of society, because this is not possible. Out of every ten letters of this kind, nine will allege, as the reason of the writers' importunity, their desire to keep their families in such and such a "station of life." There is no real desire for the safety, the discipline, or the moral good of the children, only a panic horror of the inexpressibly pitiable calamity of their living a ledge or two lower on the molehill of the world – a calamity to be averted at any cost whatever, of struggle, anxiety, and shortening of life itself. I do not believe that any greater good could be achieved for the country, than the change in public feeling on this head, which might be brought about by a few benevolent men, undeniably in the class of "gentlemen," who would, on principle, enter into some of our commonest trades, and make them honorable; showing that it was possible for a man to retain his dignity, and remain, in the best sense, a gentleman, though part of his time was every day occupied in manual labor, or even in serving customers over a counter. I do not in the least see why courtesy, and gravity, and sympathy with the feelings of others, and courage, and truth, and piety, and what else goes to make up a gentleman's character, should not be found behind a counter as well as elsewhere, if they were demanded, or even hoped for, there.

Let us suppose, then, that the man's way of life and manner of work have been discreetly chosen; then the next thing to be required is, that he do not over-work himself therein. I am not going to say anything here about the various errors in our systems of society and commerce, which appear (I am not sure if they ever do more than appear) to force us to over-work ourselves merely that we may live; nor about the still more fruitful cause of unhealthy toil – the incapability, in many men, of being content with the little that is indeed necessary to their happiness. I have only a word or two to say about one special cause of over-work – the ambitious desire of doing great or clever things, and the hope of accomplishing them by immense efforts: hope as vain as it is pernicious; not only making men over-work themselves, but rendering all the work they do unwholesome to them. I say it is a vain hope, and let the reader be assured of this (it is a truth all-important to the best interests of humanity). *No great intellectual thing was ever done by great effort*; a great thing can only be done by a great man, and he does it *without* effort. Nothing is, at present, less understood by us than this – nothing is more necessary to be understood. Let me try to say it as clearly, and explain it as fully as I may.

I have said no great *intellectual* thing: for I do not mean the assertion to extend to things moral. On the contrary, it seems to me that just because we are intended, as long as we live, to be in a state of intense moral effort, we are *not* intended to be in intense physical or intellectual effort. Our full energies are to be given to the soul's work – to the great fight with the Dragon – the taking the kingdom of heaven by force. But the body's work and head's work are to be done quietly, and comparatively without effort. Neither limbs nor brain are ever to be strained to their utmost; that is not the way in which the greatest quantity of work is to be got out of them: they are never to be worked furiously, but with tranquillity and constancy. We are to follow the plough from sunrise to sunset, but not to pull in race-boats at the twilight: we shall get no fruit of that kind of work, only disease of the heart.

How many pangs would be spared to thousands, if this great truth and law were but once sincerely, humbly understood, – that if a great thing can be done at all, it can be done easily; that, when it is needed to be done, there is perhaps only one man in the world who can do it; but *he* can do it without any trouble – without more trouble, that is, than it costs small people to do small things; nay, perhaps, with less. And yet what truth lies more openly on the surface of all human phenomena? Is not the evidence of Ease on the very front of all the greatest works in existence? Do they not say plainly to us, not, "there has been a great *effort* here," but, "there has been a great *power* here"? It is not the weariness of mortality, but the strength of divinity, which we have to recognise in all mighty things; and that is just what we now *never* recognise, but think that we are to do great things, by help of iron bars and perspiration: – alas! we shall do nothing that way but lose some pounds of our own weight.

Yet, let me not be misunderstood, nor this great truth be supposed anywise resolvable into the favorite dogma of young men, that they need not work if they have genius. The fact is, that a man of genius is always far more ready to work than other people, and gets so much more good from the work that he does, and is often so little conscious of the inherent divinity in himself, that he is very apt to ascribe all his capacity to his work, and to tell those who ask how he came to be what he is: "If I *am* anything, which I much doubt, I made myself so merely by labor." This was Newton's way of talking, and I suppose it would be the general tone of men whose genius had been devoted to the physical sciences. Genius in the Arts must commonly be more self-conscious, but in whatever field, it will always be distinguished by its perpetual, steady, well-directed, happy, and faithful labor in accumulating and disciplining its powers, as well as by its gigantic, incommunicable facility in exercising them. Therefore, literally, it is no man's business whether he has genius or not: work he must, whatever he is, but quietly and steadily; and the natural and unforced results of such work will be always the things that God meant him to do, and will be his best. No agonies nor heart-rendings will enable him to do any better. If he be a great man, they will be great things; if a small man, small things; but always, if thus peacefully done, good and right; always, if restlessly and ambitiously done, false, hollow, and despicable.

Then the third thing needed was, I said, that a man should be a good judge of his work; and this chiefly that he may not be dependent upon popular opinion for the manner of doing it, but also that he may have the just encouragement of the sense of progress, and an honest consciousness of victory: how else can he become

"That awful independent on to-morrow,
Whose yesterdays look backwards with a smile."

I am persuaded that the real nourishment and help of such a feeling as this is nearly unknown to half the workmen of the present day. For whatever appearance of self-complacency there may be in their outward bearing, it is visible enough, by their feverish jealousy of each other, how little confidence they have in the sterling value of their several doings. Conceit may puff a man up, but never prop him up; and there is too visible distress and hopelessness in men's aspects to admit of the supposition that they have any stable support of faith in themselves.

I have stated these principles generally, because there is no branch of labor to which they do not apply: But there is one in which our ignorance or forgetfulness of them has caused an incalculable amount of suffering: and I would endeavor now to reconsider them with especial reference to it, – the branch of the Arts.

In general, the men who are employed in the Arts have freely chosen their profession, and suppose themselves to have special faculty for it; yet, as a body, they are not happy men. For which this seems to me the reason, that they are expected, and themselves expect, to make their bread *by being clever* – not by steady or quiet work; and are, therefore, for the most part, trying to be clever, and so living in an utterly false state of mind and action.

This is the case, to the same extent, in no other profession or employment. A lawyer may indeed suspect that, unless he has more wit than those around him, he is not likely to advance in his profession; but he will not be always thinking how he is to display his wit. He will generally understand, early in his career, that wit must be left to take care of itself, and that it is hard knowledge of law and vigorous examination and collation of the facts of every case entrusted to him, which his clients will mainly demand; this it is which he has to be paid for; and this is healthy and measurable labor, payable by the hour. If he happen to have keen natural perception and quick wit, these will come into play in their due time and place, but he will not think of them as his chief power; and if he have them not, he may still hope that industry and conscientiousness may enable him to rise in his profession without them. Again in the case of clergymen: that they are sorely tempted to display their eloquence or wit, none who know their own hearts will deny, but then they *know* this to *be* a temptation: they never would suppose that cleverness was all that was to be expected from them, or would sit down deliberately to write a clever sermon: even the dullest or vainest of them would throw some veil over their vanity, and pretend to some profitableness of purpose in what they did. They would not openly ask of their hearers – Did you think my sermon ingenious, or my language poetical? They would early understand that they were not paid for being ingenious, nor called to be so, but to preach truth; that if they happened to possess wit, eloquence, or originality, these would appear and be of service in due time, but were not to be continually sought after or exhibited: and if it should happen that they had them not, they might still be serviceable pastors without them.

Not so with the unhappy artist. No one expects any honest or useful work of him; but every one expects him to be ingenious. Originality, dexterity, invention, imagination, every thing is asked of him except what alone is to be had for asking – honesty and sound work, and the due discharge of his function as a painter. What function? asks the reader in some surprise. He may well ask; for I suppose few painters have any idea what their function is, or even that they have any at all.

And yet surely it is not so difficult to discover. The faculties, which when a man finds in himself, he resolves to be a painter, are, I suppose, intenseness of observation and facility of imitation. The man is created an observer and an imitator; and his function is to convey knowledge to his fellow-men, of such things as cannot be taught otherwise than ocularly. For a long time this function remained a religious one: it was to impress upon the popular mind the reality of the objects of faith, and the truth of the histories of Scripture, by giving visible form to both. That function has now passed away, and none has as yet taken its place. The painter has no profession, no purpose. He is an idler on the earth, chasing the shadows of his own fancies.

But he was never meant to be this. The sudden and universal Naturalism, or inclination to copy ordinary natural objects, which manifested itself among the painters of Europe, at the moment when the invention of printing superseded their legendary labors, was no false instinct. It was misunderstood and misapplied, but it came at the right time, and has maintained itself through all kinds of abuse; presenting in the recent schools of landscape, perhaps only the first fruits of its power. That instinct was urging every painter in Europe at the same moment to his true duty – *the faithful representation of all objects of historical interest, or of natural beauty existent at the period*; representations such as might at once aid the advance of the sciences, and keep faithful record of every monument of past ages which was likely to be swept away in the approaching eras of revolutionary change.

The instinct came, as I said, exactly at the right moment; and let the reader consider what amount and kind of general knowledge might by this time have been possessed by the nations of Europe, had their painters understood and obeyed it. Suppose that, after disciplining themselves so as to be able to draw, with unerring precision, each the particular kind of subject in which he most delighted, they had separated into two great armies of historians and naturalists; – that the first had painted with absolute faithfulness every edifice, every city, every battle-field, every scene of the slightest historical interest, precisely and completely rendering their aspect at the time; and that their companions, according to their several powers, had painted with like fidelity the plants and animals, the natural scenery, and the atmospheric phenomena of every country on the earth – suppose that a faithful and complete record were now in our museums of every building destroyed by war, or time, or innovation, during these last 200 years – suppose that each recess of every mountain chain of Europe had been penetrated, and its rocks drawn with such accuracy that the geologist's diagram was no longer necessary – suppose that every tree of the forest had been drawn in its noblest aspect, every beast of the field in its savage life – that all these gatherings were already in our national galleries, and that the painters of the present day were laboring, happily and earnestly, to multiply them, and put such means of knowledge more and more within reach of the common people –

would not that be a more honorable life for them, than gaining precarious bread by "bright effects?" They think not, perhaps. They think it easy, and therefore contemptible, to be truthful; they have been taught so all their lives. But it is not so, whoever taught it them. It is most difficult, and worthy of the greatest men's greatest effort, to render, as it should be rendered, the simplest of the natural features of the earth; but also be it remembered, no man is confined to the simplest; each may look out work for himself where he chooses, and it will be strange if he cannot find something hard enough for him. The excuse is, however, one of the lips only; for every painter knows that when he draws back from the attempt to render nature as she is, it is oftener in cowardice than in disdain.

I must leave the reader to pursue this subject for himself; I have not space to suggest to him the tenth part of the advantages which would follow, both to the painter from such an understanding of his mission, and to the whole people, in the results of his labor. Consider how the man himself would be elevated: how content he would become, how earnest, how full of all accurate and noble knowledge, how free from envy – knowing creation to be infinite, feeling at once the value of what he did, and yet the nothingness. Consider the advantage to the people; the immeasurably larger interest given to art itself; the easy, pleasurable, and perfect knowledge conveyed by it, in every subject; the far greater number of men who might be healthily and profitably occupied with it as a means of livelihood; the useful direction of myriads of inferior talents, now left fading away in misery. Conceive all this, and then look around at our exhibitions, and behold the "cattle pieces," and "sea pieces," and "fruit pieces," and "family pieces;" the eternal brown cows in ditches, and white sails in squalls, and sliced lemons in saucers, and foolish faces in simpers; – and try to feel what we are, and what we might have been.

Take a single instance in one branch of archæology. Let those who are interested in the history of religion consider what a treasure we should now have possessed, if, instead of painting pots, and vegetables, and drunken peasantry, the most accurate painters of the seventeenth and eighteenth centuries had been set to copy, line for line, the religious and domestic sculpture on the German, Flemish, and French cathedrals and castles; and if every building destroyed in the French or in any other subsequent revolution, had thus been drawn in all its parts with the same precision with which Gerard Douw or Mieris paint bas-reliefs of Cupids. Consider, even now, what incalculable treasure is still left in ancient bas-reliefs, full of every kind of legendary interest, of subtle expression, of priceless evidence as to the character, feelings habits, histories, of past generations, in neglected and shattered churches and domestic buildings, rapidly disappearing over the whole of Europe – treasure which, once lost, the labor of all men living cannot bring back again; and then look at the myriads of men, with skill enough, if they had but the commonest schooling, to record all this faithfully, who are making their bread by drawing dances of naked women from academy models, or idealities of chivalry fitted out with Wardour Street armor, or eternal scenes from Gil Blas, Don Quixote, and the Vicar of Wakefield, or mountain sceneries with young idiots of Londoners wearing Highland bonnets and brandishing rifles in the foregrounds. Do but think of these things in the breadth of their inexpressible imbecility, and then go and stand before that broken bas-relief in the southern gate of Lincoln Cathedral, and see if there is no fibre of the heart in you that will break too.

But is there to be no place left, it will be indignantly asked, for imagination and invention, for poetical power, or love of ideal beauty? Yes; the highest, the noblest place – that which these only can attain when they are all used in the cause, and with the aid of truth. Wherever imagination and sentiment are, they will either show themselves without forcing, or, if capable of artificial development, the kind of training which such a school of art would give them would be the best they could receive. The infinite absurdity and failure of our present training consists mainly in this, that we do not rank imagination and invention high enough, and suppose that they *can* be taught. Throughout every sentence that I ever have written, the reader will find the same rank attributed to these powers, – the rank of a purely divine gift, not to be attained, increased, or in any wise modified by teaching, only in various ways capable of being concealed or quenched. Understand this thoroughly; know once for all, that a poet on canvas is exactly the same species of creature as a poet in song, and nearly every error in our methods of teaching will be done away with. For who among us now thinks of bringing men up to be poets? – of producing poets by any kind of general recipe or method of cultivation? Suppose even that we see in youth that which we hope may, in its development, become a power of this kind, should we instantly, supposing that we wanted to make a poet of him, and nothing else, forbid him all quiet, steady, rational labor? Should we force him to perpetual spinning of new crudities out of his boyish brain, and set before him, as the only objects of his study, the laws of versification which criticism has supposed itself to discover in the works of previous writers? Whatever gifts the boy had, would much be likely to come of them so treated? unless, indeed, they were so great as to break through all such snares of falsehood and vanity, and build their own foundation in spite of us; whereas if, as in cases numbering millions against units, the natural gifts were too weak to do this, could any thing come of such training but utter inanity and spuriousness of the whole man? But if we had sense, should we not rather restrain and bridle the first flame of invention in early youth, heaping material on it as one would on the first sparks and tongues of a fire which we desired to feed into greatness? Should we not educate the whole intellect into general strength, and all the affections into warmth and honesty, and look to heaven for the rest? This, I say, we should have sense enough to do, in order to produce a poet in words: but, it being required to produce a poet on canvas, what is our way of setting to work? We begin, in all probability, by telling the youth of fifteen or sixteen, that Nature is full of faults, and that he is to improve her; but that Raphael is perfection, and that the more he copies Raphael the better; that after much copying of Raphael, he is to try what he can do himself in a Raphaelesque, but yet original, manner: that is to say, he is to try to do something very clever, all out of his own head, but yet this clever something is to be properly subjected to Raphaelesque rules, is to have a principal light occupying one-seventh of its space, and a principle shadow occupying one-third of the same; that no two people's heads in the picture are to be turned the same way, and that all the personages represented are to possess ideal beauty of the highest order, which ideal beauty consists partly in a Greek outline of nose, partly in proportions expressible in decimal fractions between the lips and chin; but partly also in that degree of improvement which the youth of sixteen is to bestow upon God's work in general. This I say is the kind of teaching which through various channels, Royal Academy lecturings, press criticisms, public enthusiasm, and not least by solid weight of gold, we give to our young men. And we wonder we have no painters!

But we do worse than this. Within the last few years some sense of the real tendency of such teaching has appeared in some of our younger painters. It only *could* appear in the younger ones, our older men having become familiarised with the false system, or else having passed through it and forgotten it, not well knowing the degree of harm they had sustained. This sense appeared, among our youths, – increased, – matured into resolute action. Necessarily, to exist at all, it needed the support both of strong instincts and of considerable self-confidence, otherwise it must at once have been borne down by the weight of general authority and received canon law. Strong instincts are apt to make men strange, and rude; self-confidence, however well founded, to give much of what they do or say the appearance of impertinence. Look at the self-confidence of Wordsworth, stiffening every other sentence of his prefaces into defiance; there is no more of it than was needed to enable him to do his work, yet it is not a little ungraceful here and there. Suppose this stubbornness and self-trust in a youth, laboring in an art of which the executive part is confessedly to be best learnt from masters, and we shall hardly wonder that much of his work has a certain awkwardness and stiffness in it, or that he should be regarded with disfavor by many, even the most temperate, of the judges trained in the system he was breaking through, and with utter contempt and reprobation by the envious and the dull. Consider, farther, that the particular system to be overthrown was, in the present case, one of which the main characteristic was the pursuit of beauty at the expense of manliness and truth; and it will seem likely, *à priori*, that the men intended successfully to resist the influence of such a system should be endowed with little natural sense of beauty, and thus rendered dead to the temptation it presented. Summing up these conditions, there is surely little cause for surprise that pictures painted, in a temper of resistance, by exceedingly young men, of stubborn instincts and positive self-trust, and with little natural perception of beauty, should not be calculated, at the first glance, to win us from works enriched by plagiarism, polished by convention, invested with all the attractiveness of artificial grace, and recommended to our respect by established authority.

We should, however, on the other hand, have anticipated, that in proportion to the strength of character required for the effort, and to the absence of distracting sentiments, whether respect for precedent, or affection for ideal beauty, would be the energy exhibited in the pursuit of the special objects which the youths proposed to themselves, and their success in attaining them.

All this has actually been the case, but in a degree which it would have been impossible to anticipate. That two youths, of the respective ages of eighteen and twenty, should have conceived for themselves a totally independent and sincere method of study, and enthusiastically persevered in it against every kind of dissuasion and opposition, is strange enough; that in the third or fourth year of their efforts they should have produced works in many parts not inferior to the best of Albert Durer, this is perhaps not less strange. But the loudness and universality of the howl which the common critics of the press have raised against them, the utter absence of all generous help or encouragement from those who can both measure their toil and appreciate their success, and the shrill, shallow laughter of those who can do neither the one nor the other, – these are strangest of all – unimaginable unless they had been experienced.

And as if these were not enough, private malice is at work against them, in its own small, slimy way. The very day after I had written my second letter to the Times in the defence of the Pre-Raphaelites, I received an anonymous letter respecting one of them, from some person apparently hardly capable of spelling, and about as vile a specimen of petty malignity as ever blotted paper. I think it well that the public should know this, and so get some insight into the sources of the spirit which is at work against these men – how first roused it is difficult to say, for one would hardly have thought that mere eccentricity in young artists could have excited an hostility so determined and so cruel; – hostility which hesitated at no assertion, however impudent. That of the "absence of perspective" was one of the most curious pieces of the hue and cry which began with the Times, and died away in feeble maundering in the Art Union; I contradicted it in the Times – I here contradict it directly for the second time. There was not a single error in perspective in three out of the four pictures in question. But if otherwise, would it have been anything remarkable in them? I doubt, if with the exception of the pictures of David Roberts, there were one architectural drawing in perspective on the walls of the Academy; I never met but with two men in my life who knew enough of perspective to draw a Gothic arch in a retiring plane, so that its lateral dimensions and curvatures might be calculated to scale from the drawing. Our architects certainly do not, and it was but the other day that, talking to one of the most distinguished among them, the author of several most valuable works, I found he actually did not know how to draw a circle in perspective. And in this state of general science our writers for the press take it upon them to tell us, that the forest trees in Mr. Hunt's *Sylvia*, and the bunches of lilies in Mr. Collins's *Convent Thoughts*, are out of perspective.[1]

It might not, I think, in such circumstances, have been ungraceful or unwise in the Academicians themselves to have defended their young pupils, at least by the contradiction of statements directly false respecting them,[2] and the direction of the mind and sight of the public to such real merit as they possess. If Sir Charles Eastlake, Mulready, Edwin and Charles Landseer, Cope, and Dyce would each of them simply state their own private opinion respecting their paintings, sign it and publish it, I believe the act would be of more service to English art than any thing the Academy has done since it was founded. But as I cannot hope for this, I can only ask the public to give their pictures careful examination, and look at them at once with the indulgence and the respect which I have endeavored to show they deserve.

Yet let me not be misunderstood. I have adduced them only as examples of the kind of study which I would desire to see substituted for that of our modern schools, and of singular success in certain characters, finish of detail, and brilliancy of color. What faculties, higher than imitative, may be in these men, I do not yet venture to say; but I do say that if they exist, such faculties will manifest themselves in due time all the more forcibly because they have received training so severe.

For it is always to be remembered that no one mind is like another, either in its powers or perceptions; and while the main principles of training must be the same for all, the result in each will be as various as the kinds of truth which each will apprehend; therefore, also, the modes of effort, even in men whose inner principles and final aims are exactly the same. Suppose, for instance, two men, equally honest, equally industrious, equally impressed with a humble desire to render some part of what they saw in nature faithfully; and, otherwise trained in convictions such as I have above endeavored to induce. But one of them is quiet in temperament, has a feeble memory, no invention, and excessively keen sight. The other is impatient in temperament, has a memory which nothing escapes, an invention which never rests, and is comparatively near-sighted.

Set them both free in the same field in a mountain valley. One sees everything, small and large, with almost the same clearness; mountains and grasshoppers alike; the leaves on the branches, the veins in the pebbles, the bubbles in the stream: but he can remember nothing, and invent nothing. Patiently he sets himself to his mighty task; abandoning at once all thoughts of seizing transient effects, or giving general impressions of that which his eyes present to him in microscopical dissection, he chooses some small portion out of the infinite scene, and calculates with courage the number of weeks which must elapse before he can do justice to the intensity of his perceptions, or the fulness of matter in his subject.

Meantime, the other has been watching the change of the clouds, and the march of the light along the mountain sides; he beholds the entire scene in broad, soft masses of true gradation, and the very feebleness of his sight is in some sort an advantage to him, in making him more sensible of the aërial mystery of distance, and hiding from him the multitudes of circumstances which it would have been impossible for him to represent. But there is not one change in the casting of the jagged shadows along the hollows of the hills, but it is fixed on his mind for ever; not a flake of spray has broken from the sea of cloud about their bases, but he has watched it as it melts away, and could recall it to its lost place in heaven by the slightest effort of his thoughts. Not only so, but thousands and thousands of such images, of older scenes, remain congregated in his mind, each mingling in new associations with those now visibly passing before him, and these again confused with other images of his own ceaseless, sleepless imagination, flashing by in sudden troops. Fancy how his paper will be covered with stray symbols and blots, and undecipherable shorthand: – as for his sitting down to "draw from Nature," there was not one of the things which he wished to represent that stayed for so much as five seconds together: but none of them escaped, for all that: they are sealed up in that strange storehouse of his; he may take one of them out, perhaps, this day twenty years, and paint it in his dark room, far away. Now, observe, you may tell both of these men, when they are young, that they are to be honest, that they have an important function, and that they are not to care what Raphael did. This you may wholesomely impress on them both. But fancy the exquisite absurdity of expecting either of them to possess any of the qualities of the other.

I have supposed the feebleness of sight in the last, and of invention in the first painter, that the contrast between them might be more striking; but, with very slight modification, both the characters are real. Grant to the first considerable inventive power, with exquisite sense of color; and give to the second, in addition to all his other faculties, the eye of an eagle; and the first is John Everett Millais, the second Joseph Mallard William Turner.

They are among the few men who have defied all false teaching, and have, therefore, in great measure, done justice to the gifts with which they were entrusted. They stand at opposite poles, marking culminating points of art in both directions; between them, or in various relations to them, we may class five or six more living artists who, in like manner, have done justice to their powers. I trust that I may be pardoned for naming them, in order that the reader may know how the strong innate genius in each has been invariably accompanied with the same humility, earnestness, and industry in study.

It is hardly necessary to point out the earnestness or humility in the works of William Hunt; but it may be so to suggest the high value they possess as records of English rural life, and *still* life. Who is there who for a moment could contend with him in the unaffected, yet humorous truth with which he has painted our peasant children? Who is there who does not sympathize with him in the simple love with which he dwells on the brightness and bloom of our summer fruit and flowers? And yet there is something to be regretted concerning him: why should he be allowed continually to paint the same bunches of hot-house grapes, and supply to the Water Color Society a succession of pineapples with the regularity of a Covent Garden fruiterer? He has of late discovered that primrose banks are lovely; but there are other things grow wild besides primroses: what undreamt-of loveliness might he not bring back to us, if he would lose himself for a summer in Highland foregrounds; if he would paint the heather as it grows, and the foxglove and the harebell as they nestle in the clefts of the rocks, and the mosses and bright lichens of the rocks themselves. And then, cross to the Jura, and bring back a piece of Jura pasture in spring; with the gentians in their earliest blue, and the soldanelle beside the fading snow! And return again, and paint a gray wall of Alpine crag, with budding roses crowning it like a wreath of rubies. That is what he was meant to do in this world; not to paint bouquets in china vases.

I have in various other places expressed my sincere respect for the works of Samuel Prout: his shortness of sight has necessarily prevented their possessing delicacy of finish or fulness of minor detail; but I think that those of no other living artist furnish an example so striking of innate and special instinct, sent to do a particular work at the exact and only period when it was possible. At the instant when peace had been established all over Europe, but when neither national character nor national architecture had as yet been seriously changed by promiscuous intercourse or modern "improvement;" when, however, nearly every ancient and beautiful building had been long left in a state of comparative neglect, so that its aspect of partial ruinousness, and of separation from recent active life, gave to every edifice a peculiar interest – half sorrowful, half sublime; – at that moment Prout was trained among the rough rocks and simple cottages of Cornwall, until his eye was accustomed to follow with delight the rents and breaks, and irregularities which, to another man, would have been offensive; and then, gifted with infinite readiness in composition, but also with infinite affection for the kind of subjects he had to portray, he was sent to preserve, in an almost innumerable series of drawings, *every one made on the spot*, the aspect borne, at the beginning of the nineteenth century, by cities which, in a few years more, rekindled wars, or unexpected prosperities, were to ravage, or renovate, into nothingness.

It seems strange to pass from Prout to John Lewis; but there is this fellowship between them, that both seem to have been intended to appreciate the characters of foreign countries more than of their own – nay, to have been born in England chiefly that the excitement of strangeness might enhance to them the interest of the scenes they had to represent. I believe John Lewis to have done more entire justice to all his powers (and they are magnificent ones) than any other man amongst us. His mission was evidently to portray the comparatively animal life of the southern and eastern families of mankind. For this he was prepared in a somewhat singular way – by being led to study, and endowed with altogether peculiar apprehension of, the most sublime characters of animals themselves. Rubens, Rembrandt, Snyders, Tintoret, and Titian, have all, in various ways, drawn wild beasts magnificently; but they have in some sort humanized or demonized them, making them either ravenous fiends or educated beasts, that would draw cars, and had respect for hermits. The sullen isolation of the brutal nature; the dignity and quietness of the mighty limbs; the shaggy mountainous power, mingled with grace, as of a flowing stream; the stealthy restraint of strength and wrath in every soundless motion of the gigantic frame; all this seems never to have been seen, much less drawn, until Lewis drew and himself engraved a series of animal subjects, now many years ago. Since then, he has devoted himself to the portraiture of those European and Asiatic races, among whom the refinements of civilization exist without its laws or its energies, and in whom the fierceness, indolence, and subtlety of animal nature are associated with brilliant imagination and strong affections. To this task he has brought not only intense perception of the kind of character, but powers of artistical composition like those of the great Venetians, displaying, at the same time, a refinement of drawing almost miraculous, and appreciable only, as the minutiæ of nature itself are appreciable, by the help of the microscope. The value, therefore, of his works, as records of the aspect of the scenery and inhabitants of the south of Spain and of the East, in the earlier part of the nineteenth century, is quite above all estimate.

I hardly know how to speak of Mulready: in delicacy and completion of drawing, and splendor of color, he takes place beside John Lewis and the pre-Raphaelites; but he has, throughout his career, displayed no definiteness in choice of subject. He must be named among the painters who have studied with industry, and have made themselves great by doing so; but having obtained a consummate method of execution, he has thrown it away on subjects either altogether uninteresting, or above his powers, or unfit for pictorial representation. "The Cherry Woman," exhibited in 1850, may be named as an example of the first kind; the "Burchell and Sophia" of the second (the character of Sir William Thornhill being utterly missed); the "Seven Ages" of the third; for this subject cannot be painted. In the written passage, the thoughts are progressive and connected; in the picture they must be co-existent, and yet separate; nor can all the characters of the ages be rendered in painting at all. One may represent the soldier at the cannon's mouth, but one cannot paint the "bubble reputation" which he seeks. Mulready, therefore, while he has always produced exquisite pieces of painting, has failed in doing anything which can be of true or extensive use. He has, indeed, understood how to discipline his genius, but never how to direct it.

Edwin Landseer is the last painter but one whom I shall name: I need not point out to any one acquainted with his earlier works, the labor, or watchfulness of nature which they involve, nor need I do more than allude to the peculiar faculties of his mind. It will at once be granted that the highest merits of his pictures are throughout found in those parts of them which are least like what had before been accomplished; and that it was not by the study of Raphael that he attained his eminent success, but by a healthy love of Scotch terriers.

None of these painters, however, it will be answered, afford examples of the rise of the highest imaginative power out of close study of matters of fact. Be it remembered, however, that the imaginative power, in its magnificence, is not to be found every day. Lewis has it in no mean degree; but we cannot hope to find it at its highest more than once in an age. We *have* had it once, and must be content.

Towards the close of the last century, among the various drawings executed, according to the quiet manner of the time, in greyish blue, with brown foregrounds, some began to be noticed as exhibiting rather more than ordinary diligence and delicacy, signed W. Turner.[3] There was nothing, however, in them at all indicative of genius, or even of more than ordinary talent, unless in some of the subjects a large perception of space, and excessive clearness and decision in the arrangement of masses. Gradually and cautiously the blues became mingled with delicate green, and then with gold; the browns in the foreground became first more positive, and then were slightly mingled with other local colors; while the touch, which had at first been heavy and broken, like that of the ordinary drawing masters of the time, grew more and more refined and expressive, until it lost itself in a method of execution often too delicate for the eye to follow, rendering, with a precision before unexampled, both the texture and the form of every object. The style may be considered as perfectly formed about the year 1800, and it remained unchanged for twenty years.

During that period the painter had attempted, and with more or less success had rendered, every order of landscape subject, but always on the same principle, subduing the colors of nature into a harmony of which the key-notes are greyish green and brown; pure blues and delicate golden yellows being admitted in small quantity, as the lowest and highest limits of shade and light: and bright local colors in extremely small quantity in figures or other minor accessories.

Pictures executed on such a system are not, properly speaking, works in *color* at all; they are studies of light and shade, in which both the shade and the distance are rendered in the general hue which best expresses their attributes of coolness and transparency; and the lights and the foreground are executed in that which best expresses their warmth and solidity. This advantage may just as well be taken as not, in studies of light and shadow to be executed with the hand: but the use of two, three, or four colors, always in the same relations and places, does not in the least constitute the work a study of color, any more than the brown engravings of the Liber Studiorum; nor would the idea of color be in general more present to the artist's mind, when he was at work on one of these drawings, than when he was using pure brown in the mezzotint engraving. But the idea of space, warmth, and freshness being not successfully expressible in a single tint, and perfectly expressible by the admission of three or four, he allows himself this advantage when it is possible, without in the least embarrassing himself with the actual color of the objects to be represented. A stone in the fore ground might in nature have been cold grey, but it will be drawn nevertheless of a rich brown, because it is in the foreground; a hill in the distance might in nature be purple with heath, or golden with furze; but it will be drawn nevertheless of a cool grey, because it is in the distance.

This at least was the general theory, – carried out with great severity in many, both of the drawings and pictures executed by him during the period: in others more or less modified by the cautious introduction of color, as the painter felt his liberty increasing; for the system was evidently never considered as final, or as anything more than a means of progress: the conventional, easily manageable color, was visibly adopted, only that his mind might be at perfect liberty to address itself to the acquirement of the first and most necessary knowledge in all art –

that of form. But as form, in landscape, implies vast bulk and space, the use of the tints which enabled him best to express them, was actually auxiliary to the mere drawing; and, therefore, not only permissible, but even necessary, while more brilliant or varied tints were never indulged in, except when they might be introduced without the slightest danger of diverting his mind for an instant from his principal object. And, therefore, it will be generally found in the works of this period, that exactly in proportion to the importance and general toil of the composition, is the severity of the tint; and that the play of color begins to show itself first in slight and small drawings, where he felt that he could easily secure all that he wanted in form.

Thus the "Crossing the Brook," and such other elaborate and large compositions, are actually painted in nothing but grey, brown, and blue, with a point or two of severe local color in the figures; but in the minor drawings, tender passages of complicated color occur not unfrequently in easy places; and even before the year 1800 he begins to introduce it with evident joyfulness and longing in his rude and simple studies, just as a child, if it could be supposed to govern itself by a fully developed intellect, would cautiously, but with infinite pleasure, add now and then a tiny dish of fruit or other dangerous luxury to the simple order of its daily fare. Thus, in the foregrounds of his most severe drawings, we not unfrequently find him indulging in the luxury of a peacock; and it is impossible to express the joyfulness with which he seems to design its graceful form, and deepen with soft pencilling the bloom of its blue, after he has worked through the stern detail of his almost colorless drawing. A rainbow is another of his most frequently permitted indulgences; and we find him very early allowing the edges of his evening clouds to be touched with soft rose-color or gold; while, whenever the hues of nature in anywise fall into his system, and can be caught without a dangerous departure from it, he instantly throws his whole soul into the faithful rendering of them. Thus the usual brown tones of his foreground become warmed into sudden vigor, and are varied and enhanced with indescribable delight, when he finds himself by the shore of a moorland stream, where they truly express the stain of its golden rocks, and the darkness of its clear, Cairngorm-like pools, and the usual serenity of his aërial blue is enriched into the softness and depth of the sapphire, when it can deepen the distant slumber of some Highland lake, or temper the gloomy shadows of the evening upon its hills.

The system of his color being thus simplified, he could address all the strength of his mind to the accumulation of facts of form; his choice of subject, and his methods of treatment, are therefore as various as his color is simple; and it is not a little difficult to give the reader who is unacquainted with his works, an idea either of their infinitude of aims, on the one hand, or of the kind of feeling which prevades them all, on the other. No subject was too low or too high for him; we find him one day hard at work on a cock and hen, with their family of chickens in a farm-yard; and bringing all the refinement of his execution into play to express the texture of the plumage; next day, he is drawing the Dragon of Colchis. One hour he is much interested in a gust of wind blowing away an old woman's cap; the next he is painting the fifth plague of Egypt. Every landscape painter before him had acquired distinction by confining his efforts to one class of subject. Hobbima painted oaks; Ruysdael, waterfalls and copses; Cuyp, river or meadow scenes in quiet afternoons; Salvator and Poussin, such kind of mountain scenery as people could conceive, who lived in towns in the seventeenth century. But I am well persuaded that if all the works of Turner, up to the year 1820, were divided into classes (as he has himself divided them in the Liber Studiorum), no preponderance could be assigned to one class over another. There is architecture, including a large number of formal "gentlemen's seats," I suppose drawings commissioned by the owners; then lowland pastoral scenery of every kind, including nearly all farming operations, – ploughing, harrowing, hedging and ditching, felling trees, sheep-washing, and I know not what else; then all kinds of town life – court-yards of inns, starting of mail coaches, interiors of shops, house-buildings, fairs, elections, &c.; then all kinds of inner domestic life – interiors of rooms, studies of costumes, of still life, and heraldry, including multitudes of symbolical vignettes; then marine scenery of every kind, full of local incident; every kind of boat and method of fishing for particular fish, being specifically drawn, round the whole coast of England; – pilchard fishing at St. Ives, whiting fishing at Margate, herring at Loch Fyne; and all kinds of shipping, including studies of every separate part of the vessels, and many marine battle-pieces, two in particular of Trafalgar, both of high importance, – one of the Victory after the battle, now in Greenwich Hospital; another of the Death of Nelson, in his own gallery; then all kinds of mountain scenery, some idealised into compositions, others of definite localities; together with classical compositions, Romes and Carthages and such others, by the myriad, with mythological, historical, or allegorical figures, – nymphs, monsters, and spectres; heroes and divinities.[4]

What general feeling, it may be asked incredulously, can possibly pervade all this? This, the greatest of all feelings – an utter forgetfulness of self. Throughout the whole period with which we are at present concerned, Turner appears as a man of sympathy absolutely infinite – a sympathy so all-embracing, that I know nothing but that of Shakespeare comparable with it. A soldier's wife resting by the roadside is not beneath it; Rizpah, the daughter of Aiah, watching the dead bodies of her sons, not above it. Nothing can possibly be so mean as that it will not interest his whole mind, and carry away his whole heart; nothing so great or solemn but that he can raise himself into harmony with it; and it is impossible to prophesy of him at any moment, whether, the next, he will be in laughter or in tears.

This is the root of the man's greatness; and it follows as a matter of course that this sympathy must give him a subtle power of expression, even of the characters of mere material things, such as no other painter ever possessed. The man who can best feel the difference between rudeness and tenderness in humanity, perceives also more difference between the branches of an oak and a willow than any one else would; and therefore, necessarily the most striking character of the drawings themselves is the speciality of whatever they represent – the thorough stiffness of what is stiff, and grace of what is graceful, and vastness of what is vast; but through and beyond all this, the condition of the mind of the painter himself is easily enough discoverable by comparison of a large number of the drawings. It is singularly serene and peaceful: in itself quite passionless, though entering with ease into the external passion which it contemplates. By the effort of its will it sympathises with tumult or distress, even in their extremes, but there is no tumult, no sorrow in itself, only a chastened and exquisitely peaceful cheerfulness, deeply meditative; touched without loss of its own perfect balance, by sadness on the one side, and stooping to playfulness upon the other. I shall never cease to regret the destruction, by fire, now several years ago, of a drawing which always seemed to me to be the perfect image of the painter's mind at this period, – the drawing of Brignal Church near Rokeby, of which a feeble idea may still be gathered from the engraving (in the Yorkshire series). The spectator stands on the "Brignal banks," looking down into the glen at twilight; the sky is still full of soft rays, though the sun is gone; and the Greta glances brightly in the valley, singing its evening-song; two white clouds, following each other, move without wind through the hollows of the ravine, and others lie couched on the far away moorlands; every leaf of the woods is still in the delicate air; a boy's kite, incapable of rising, has become entangled in their branches, he is climbing to recover it; and just behind it in the picture, almost indicated by it, the lowly church is seen in its secluded field between the rocks and the stream; and around it the low churchyard wall, and the few white stones which mark the resting places of those who can climb the rocks no more, nor hear the river sing as it passes.

There are many other existing drawings which indicate the same character of mind, though I think none so touching or so beautiful; yet they are not, as I said above, more numerous than those which express his sympathy with sublimer or more active scenes; but they are almost always marked by a tenderness of execution, and have a look of being beloved in every part of them, which shows them to be the truest expression of his own feelings.

One other characteristic of his mind at this period remains to be noticed – its reverence for talent in others. Not the reverence which acts upon the practices of men as if they were the laws of nature, but that which is ready to appreciate the power, and receive the assistance, of every mind which has been previously employed in the same direction, so far as its teaching seems to be consistent with the great text-book of nature itself. Turner thus studied almost every preceding landscape painter, chiefly Claude, Poussin, Vandevelde, Loutherbourg, and Wilson. It was probably by the Sir George Beaumonts and other feeble conventionalists of the period, that he was persuaded to devote his attention to the works of these men; and his having done so will be thought, a few scores of years hence, evidence of perhaps the greatest modesty ever shown by a man of original power. Modesty at once admirable and unfortunate, for the study of the works of Vandevelde and Claude was productive of unmixed mischief to him; he spoiled many of his marine pictures, as for instance Lord Ellesmere's, by imitation of the former; and from the latter learned a false ideal, which confirmed by the notions of Greek art prevalent in London in the beginning of this century, has manifested itself in many vulgarities in his composition pictures, vulgarities which may perhaps be best expressed by the general term "Twickenham Classicism," as consisting principally in conceptions of ancient or of rural life such as have influenced the erection of most of our suburban villas. From Nicolo Poussin and Loutherbourg he seems to have derived advantage; perhaps also from Wilson; and much in his subsequent travels from far higher men, especially Tintoret and Paul Veronese. I have myself heard him speaking with singular delight of the putting in of the beech leaves in the upper right-hand corner of Titian's Peter Martyr. I cannot in any of his works trace the slightest influence of Salvator; and I am not surprised at it, for though Salvator was a man of far higher powers than either Vandevelde or Claude, he was a wilful and gross caricaturist. Turner would condescend to be helped by feeble men, but could not be corrupted by false men. Besides, he had never himself seen classical life, and Claude was represented to him as competent authority for it. But he *had* seen mountains and torrents, and knew therefore that Salvator could not paint them.

One of the most characteristic drawings of this period fortunately bears a date, 1818, and brings us within two years of another dated drawing, no less characteristic of what I shall henceforward call Turner's Second period. It is in the possession of Mr. Hawkesworth Fawkes of Farnley, one of Turner's earliest and truest friends; and bears the inscription, unusually conspicuous, heaving itself up and down over the eminences of the foreground – "Passage of Mont Cenis. J. M. W. Turner, January 15th, 1820."

The scene is on the summit of the pass close to the hospice, or what seems to have been a hospice at that time, – I do not remember such at present, – a small square-built house, built as if partly for a fortress, with a detached flight of stone steps in front of it, and a kind of drawbridge to the door. This building, about 400 or 500 yards off, is seen in a dim, ashy grey against the light, which by help of a violent blast of mountain wind has broken through the depth of clouds which hangs upon the crags. There is no sky, properly so called, nothing but this roof of drifting cloud; but neither is there any weight of darkness – the high air is too thin for it, – all savage, howling, and luminous with cold, the massy bases of the granite hills jutting out here and there grimly through the snow wreaths. There is a desolate-looking refuge on the left, with its number 16, marked on it in long ghastly figures, and the wind is drifting the snow off the roof and through its window in a frantic whirl; the near ground is all wan with half-thawed, half-trampled snow; a diligence in front, whose horses, unable to face the wind, have turned right round with fright, its passengers struggling to escape, jammed in the window; a little farther on is another carriage off the road, some figures pushing at its wheels, and its driver at the horses' heads, pulling and lashing with all his strength, his lifted arm stretched out against the light of the distance, though too far off for the whip to be seen.

Now I am perfectly certain that any one thoroughly accustomed to the earlier works of the painter, and shown this picture for the first time, would be struck by two altogether new characters in it.

The first, a seeming enjoyment of the excitement of the scene, totally different from the contemplative philosophy with which it would formerly have been regarded. Every incident of motion and of energy is seized upon with indescribable delight, and every line of the composition animated with a force and fury which are now no longer the mere expression of a contemplated external truth, but have origin in some inherent feeling in the painter's mind.

The second, that although the subject is one in itself almost incapable of color, and although, in order to increase the wildness of the impression, all brilliant local color has been refused even where it might easily have been introduced, as in the figures; yet in the low minor key which has been chosen, the melodies of color have been elaborated to the utmost possible pitch, so as to become a leading, instead of a subordinate, element in the composition; the subdued warm hues of the granite promontories, the dull stone color of the walls of the buildings, clearly opposed, even in shade, to the grey of the snow wreaths heaped against them, and the faint greens and ghastly blues of the glacier ice, being all expressed with delicacies of transition utterly unexampled in any previous drawings.

These, accordingly, are the chief characteristics of the works of Turner's second period, as distinguished from the first, – a new energy inherent in the mind of the painter, diminishing the repose and exalting the force and fire of his conceptions, and the presence of Color, as at least an essential, and often a principal, element of design.

Not that it is impossible, or even unusual, to find drawings of serene subject, and perfectly quiet feeling, among the compositions of this period; but the repose is in them, just as the energy and tumult were in the earlier period, an external quality, which the painter images by an effort of the will: it is no longer a character inherent in himself. The "Ulleswater," in the England series, is one of those which are in most perfect peace: in the "Cowes," the silence is only broken by the dash of the boat's oars, and in the "Alnwick" by a stag drinking; but in at least nine drawings out of ten, either sky, water, or figures are in rapid motion, and the grandest drawings are almost always those which have even violent action in one or other, or in all: e. g. high force of Tees, Coventry, Llanthony, Salisbury, Llanberis, and such others.

The color is, however, a more absolute distinction; and we must return to Mr. Fawkes's collection in order to see how the change in it was effected. That such a change would take place at one time or other was of course to be securely anticipated, the conventional system of the first period being, as above stated, merely a means of Study. But the immediate cause was the journey of the year 1820. As might be guessed from the legend on the drawing above described, "Passage of Mont Cenis, January 15th, 1820," that drawing represents what happened on the day in question to the painter himself. He passed the Alps then in the winter of 1820; and either in the previous or subsequent summer, but on the same journey, he made a series of sketches on the Rhine, in body color, now in Mr. Fawkes's collection. Every one of those sketches is the almost instantaneous record of an *effect* of color or atmosphere, taken strictly from nature, the drawing and the details of every subject being comparatively subordinate, and the color nearly as principal as the light and shade had been before, – certainly the leading feature, though the light and shade are always exquisitely harmonized with it. And naturally, as the color becomes the leading object, those times of day are chosen in which it is most lovely; and whereas before, at least five out of six of Turner's drawings represented ordinary daylight, we now find his attention directed constantly to the evening: and, for the first time, we have those rosy lights upon the hills, those gorgeous falls of sun through flaming heavens, those solemn twilights, with the blue moon rising as the western sky grows dim, which have ever since been the themes of his mightiest thoughts.

I have no doubt, that the *immediate* reason of this change was the impression made upon him by the colors of the continental skies. When he first travelled on the Continent (1800), he was comparatively a young student; not yet able to draw form as he wanted, he was forced to give all his thoughts and strength to this primary object. But now he was free to receive other impressions; the time was come for perfecting his art, and the first sunset which he saw on the Rhine taught him that all previous landscape art was vain and valueless, that in comparison with natural color, the things that had been called paintings were mere ink and charcoal, and that all precedent and all authority must be cast away at once, and trodden under foot. He cast them away: the memories of Vandevelde and Claude were at once weeded out of the great mind they had encumbered; they and all the rubbish of the schools together with them; the waves of the Rhine swept them away for ever; and a new dawn rose over the rocks of the Siebengebirge.

There was another motive at work, which rendered the change still more complete. His fellow artists were already conscious enough of his superior power in drawing, and their best hope was, that he might not be able to color. They had begun to express this hope loudly enough for it to reach his ears. The engraver of one of his most important marine pictures told me, not long ago, that one day about the period in question, Turner came into his room to examine the progress of the plate, not having seen his own picture for several months. It was one of his dark early pictures, but in the foreground was a little piece of luxury, a pearly fish wrought into hues like those of an opal. He stood before the picture for some moments; then laughed, and pointed joyously to the fish; – "They say that Turner can't color!" and turned away.

Under the force of these various impulses the change was total. *Every subject thenceforth was primarily conceived in color*; and no engraving ever gave the slightest idea of any drawing of this period.

The artists who had any perception of the truth were in despair; the Beaumontites, classicalists, and "owl species" in general, in as much indignation as their dulness was capable of. They had deliberately closed their eyes to all nature, and had gone on inquiring, "Where do you put your brown tree?" A vast revelation was made to them at once, enough to have dazzled any one; but to *them*, light unendurable as incomprehensible. They "did to the moon complain," in one vociferous, unanimous, continuous "Tu whoo." Shrieking rose from all dark places at the same instant, just the same kind of shrieking that is now raised against the Pre-Raphaelites. Those glorious old Arabian Nights, how true they are! Mocking and whispering, and abuse loud and low by turns, from all the black stones beside the road, when one living soul is toiling up the hill to get the golden water. Mocking and whispering, that he may look back, and become a black stone like themselves.

Turner looked not back, but he went on in such a temper as a strong man must be in, when he is forced to walk with his fingers in his ears. He retired into himself; he could look no longer for help, or counsel, or sympathy from any one; and the spirit of defiance in which he was forced to labor led him sometimes into violences, from which the slightest expression of sympathy would have saved him. The new energy that was upon him, and the utter isolation into which he was driven, were both alike dangerous, and many drawings of the time show the evil effects of both; some of them being hasty, wild, or experimental, and others little more than magnificent expressions of defiance of public opinion.

But all have this noble virtue – they are in everything his own: there are no more reminiscences of dead masters, no more trials of skill in the manner of Claude or Poussin; every faculty of his soul is fixed upon nature only, as he saw her, or as he remembered her.

I have spoken above of his gigantic memory: it is especially necessary to notice this, in order that we may understand the kind of grasp which a man of real imagination takes of all things that are once brought within his reach – grasp thenceforth not to be relaxed for ever.

On looking over any catalogues of his works, or of particular series of them, we shall notice the recurrence of the same subject two, three, or even many times. In any other artist this would be nothing remarkable. Probably most modern landscape painters multiply a favorite subject twenty, thirty, or sixty fold, putting the shadows and the clouds in different places, and "inventing," as they are pleased to call it, a new "effect" every time. But if we examine the successions of Turner's subjects, we shall find them either the records of a succession of impressions actually perceived by him at some favorite locality, or else repetitions of one impression received in early youth, and again and again realised as his increasing powers enabled him to do better justice to it. In either case we shall find them records of *seen facts*; *never* compositions in his room to fill up a favorite outline.

For instance, every traveller, at least every traveller of thirty years' standing, must love Calais, the place where he first felt himself in a strange world. Turner evidently loved it excessively. I have never catalogued his studies of Calais, but I remember, at this moment, five: there is first the "Pas de Calais," a very large oil painting, which is what he saw in broad daylight as he crossed over, when he got near the French side. It is a careful study of French fishing boats running for the shore before the wind, with the picturesque old city in the distance. Then there is the "Calais Harbor" in the Liber Studiorum: that is what he saw just as he was going into the harbor, – a heavy brig warping out, and very likely to get in his way, or run against the pier, and bad weather coming on. Then there is the "Calais Pier," a large painting, engraved some years ago by Mr. Lupton:[5] that is what he saw when he had landed, and ran back directly to the pier to see what had become of the brig. The weather had got still worse, the fishwomen were being blown about in a distressful manner on the pier head, and some more fishing boats were running in with all speed. Then there is the "Fortrouge," Calais: that is what he saw after he had been home to Dessein's, and dined, and went out again in the evening to walk on the sands, the tide being down. He had never seen such a waste of sands before, and it made an impression on him. The shrimp girls were all scattered over them too, and moved about in white spots on the wild shore; and the storm had lulled a little, and there was a sunset – such a sunset, – and the bars of Fortrouge seen against it, skeleton-wise.

He did not paint that directly; thought over it, – painted it a long while afterwards.

Then there is the vignette in the illustrations to Scott. That is what he saw as he was going home, meditatively; and the revolving lighthouse came blazing out upon him suddenly, and disturbed him. He did not like that so much; made a vignette of it, however, when he was asked to do a bit of Calais, twenty or thirty years afterwards, having already done all the rest.

Turner never told me all this, but any one may see it if he will compare the pictures. They might, possibly, not be impressions of a single day, but of two days or three; though in all human probability they were seen just as I have stated them;[6] but they *are* records of successive impressions, as plainly written as ever traveller's diary. All of them pure veracities. Therefore immortal.

I could multiply these series almost indefinitely from the rest of his works. What is curious, some of them have a kind of private mark running through all the subjects. Thus I know three drawings of Scarborough, and all of them have a starfish in the foreground: I do not remember any others of his marine subjects which have a starfish.

The other kind of repetition – the recurrence to one early impression – is however still more remarkable. In the collection of F. H. Bale, Esq., there is a small drawing of Llanthony Abbey. It is in his boyish manner, its date probably about 1795; evidently a sketch from nature, finished at home. It had been a showery day; the hills were partially concealed by the rain, and gleams of sunshine breaking out at intervals. A man was fishing in the mountain stream. The young Turner sought a place of some shelter under the bushes; made his sketch, took great pains when he got home to imitate the rain, as he best could; added his child's luxury of a rainbow; put in the very bush under which he had taken shelter, and the fisherman, a somewhat ill-jointed and long-legged fisherman, in the courtly short breeches which were the fashion of the time.

Some thirty years afterwards, with all his powers in their strongest training, and after the total change in his feelings and principles which I have endeavored to describe, he undertook the series of "England and Wales," and in that series introduced the subject of Llanthony Abbey. And behold, he went back to his boy's sketch, and boy's thought. He kept the very bushes in their places, but brought the fisherman to the other side of the river, and put him, in somewhat less courtly dress, under their shelter, instead of himself. And then he set all his gained strength and new knowledge at work on the well-remembered shower of rain, that had fallen thirty years before, to do it better. The resultant drawing[7] is one of the very noblest of his second period.

Another of the drawings of the England series, Ulleswater, is the repetition of one in Mr. Fawkes's collection, which, by the method of its execution, I should conjecture to have been executed about the year 1808, or 1810: at all events, it is a very quiet drawing of the first period. The lake is quite calm; the western hills in grey shadow, the eastern massed in light. Helvellyn rising like a mist between them, all being mirrored in the calm water. Some thin and slightly evanescent cows are standing in the shallow water in front; a boat floats motionless about a hundred yards from the shore: the foreground is of broken rocks, with lovely pieces of copse on the right and left.

This was evidently Turner's record of a quiet evening by the shore of Ulleswater, but it was a feeble one. He could not at that time render the sunset colors: he went back to it therefore in the England series, and painted it again with his new power. The same hills are there, the same shadows, the same cows, – they had stood in his mind, on the same spot, for twenty years, – the same boat, the same rocks, only the copse is cut away – it interfered with the masses of his color: some figures are introduced bathing, and what was grey, and feeble gold in the first drawing, becomes purple, and burning rose-color in the last.

But perhaps one of the most curious examples is in the series of subjects from Winchelsea. That in the Liber Studiorum, "Winchelsea, Sussex," bears date 1812, and its figures consist of a soldier speaking to a woman, who is resting on the bank beside the road. There is another small subject, with Winchelsea in the distance, of which the engraving bears date 1817. It has *two* women with bundles, and *two* soldiers toiling along the embankment in the plain, and a baggage waggon in the distance. Neither of these seems to have satisfied him, and at last he did another for the England series, of which the engraving bears date 1830. There is now a regiment on the march; the baggage waggon is there, having got no further on in the thirteen years, but one of the women is tired, and has fainted on the bank; another is supporting her against her bundle, and giving her drink; a third sympathetic woman is added, and the two soldiers have stopped, and one is drinking from his canteen.

Nor is it merely of entire scenes, or of particular incidents, that Turner's memory is thus tenacious. The slightest passages of color or arrangement that have pleased him – the fork of a bough, the casting of a shadow, the fracture of a stone – will be taken up again and again, and strangely worked into new relations with other thoughts. There is a single sketch from nature in one of the portfolios at Farnley, of a common wood-walk on the estate, which has furnished passages to no fewer than three of the most elaborate compositions in the Liber Studiorum.

I am thus tedious in dwelling on Turner's powers of memory, because I wish it to be thoroughly seen how all his greatness, all his infinite luxuriance of invention, depends on his taking possession of everything that he sees, – on his grasping all, and losing hold of nothing, – on his forgetting himself, and forgetting nothing else. I wish it to be understood how every great man paints what he sees or did see, his greatness being indeed little else than his intense sense of fact. And thus Pre-Raphaelitism and Raphaelitism, and Turnerism, are all one and the same, so far as education can influence them. They are different in their choice, different in their faculties, but all the same in this, that Raphael himself, so far as he was great, and all who preceded or followed him who ever were great, became so by painting the truths around them as they appeared to each man's own mind, not as he had been taught to see them, except by the God who made both him and them.

There is, however, one more characteristic of Turner's second period, on which I have still to dwell, especially with reference to what has been above advanced respecting the fallacy of overtoil; namely, the magnificent ease with which all is done when it is *successfully* done. For there are one or two drawings of this time which are *not* done easily. Turner had in these set himself to do a fine thing to exhibit his powers; in the common phrase, to excel himself; so sure as he does this, the work is a failure. The worst drawings that have ever come from his hands are some of this second period, on which he has spent much time and laborious thought; drawings filled with incident from one side to the other, with skies stippled into morbid blue, and warm lights set against them in violent contrast; one of Bamborough Castle, a large water-color, may be named as an example. But the truly noble works are those in which, without effort, he has expressed his thoughts as they came, and forgotten himself; and in these the outpouring of invention is not less miraculous than the swiftness and obedience of the mighty hand that expresses it. Any one who examines the drawings may see the evidence of this facility, in the strange freshness and sharpness of every touch of color; but when the multitude of delicate touches, with which all the aërial tones are worked, is taken into consideration, it would still appear impossible that the drawing could have been completed with *ease*, unless we had direct evidence in the matter: fortunately, it is not wanting. There is a drawing in Mr. Fawkes's collection of a man-of-war taking in stores: it is of the usual size of those of the England series, about sixteen inches by eleven: it does not appear one of the most highly finished, but is still farther removed from slightness. The hull of a first-rate occupies nearly one-half of the picture on the right, her bows towards the spectator, seen in sharp perspective from stem to stern, with all her portholes, guns, anchors, and lower rigging elaborately detailed; there are two other ships of the line in the middle distance, drawn with equal precision; a noble breezy sea dancing against their broad bows, full of delicate drawing in its waves; a store-ship beneath the hull of the larger vessel, and several other boats, and a complicated cloudy sky. It might appear no small exertion of mind to draw the detail of all this shipping down to the smallest ropes, from memory, in the drawing-room of a mansion in the middle of Yorkshire, even if considerable time had been given for the effort. But Mr. Fawkes sat beside the painter from the first stroke to the last. Turner took a piece of blank paper one morning after breakfast, outlined his ships, finished the drawing in three hours, and went out to shoot.

Let this single fact be quietly meditated upon by our ordinary painters, and they will see the truth of what was above asserted, – that if a great thing can be done at all, it can be done easily; and let them not torment themselves with twisting of compositions this way and that, and repeating, and experimenting, and scene-shifting. If a man can compose at all, he can compose at once, or rather he must compose in spite of himself. And this is the reason of that silence which I have kept in most of my works, on the subject of Composition. Many critics, especially the architects, have found fault with me for not "teaching people how to arrange masses;" for not "attributing sufficient importance to composition." Alas! I attribute far more importance to it than they do; – so much importance, that I should just as soon think of sitting down to teach a man how to write a Divina Commedia, or King Lear, as how to "compose," in the true sense, a single building or picture. The marvellous stupidity of this age of lecturers is, that they do not see that what they call "principles of composition," are mere principles of common sense in everything, as well as in pictures and buildings; – A picture is to have a principal light? Yes; and so a dinner is to have a principal dish, and an oration a principal point, and an air of music a principal note, and every man a principal object. A picture is to have harmony of relation among its parts? Yes; and so is a speech well uttered, and an action well ordered, and a company well chosen, and a ragout well mixed. Composition! As if a man were not composing every moment of his life, well or ill, and would not do it instinctively in his picture as well as elsewhere, if he could. Composition of this lower or common kind is of exactly the same importance in a picture that it is in any thing else, – no more. It is well that a man should say what he has to say in good order and sequence, but the main thing is to say it truly. And yet we go on preaching to our pupils as if to have a principal light was every thing, and so cover our academy walls with Shacabac feasts, wherein the courses are indeed well ordered, but the dishes empty.

It is not, however, only in invention that men over-work themselves, but in execution also; and here I have a word to say to the Pre-Raphaelites specially. They are working too hard. There is evidence in failing portions of their pictures, showing that they have wrought so long upon them that their very sight has failed for weariness, and that the hand refused any more to obey the heart. And, besides this, there are certain qualities of drawing which they miss from over-carefulness. For, let them be assured, there is a great truth lurking in that common desire of men to see things done in what they call a "masterly," or "bold," or "broad," manner: a truth oppressed and abused, like almost every other in this world, but an eternal one nevertheless; and whatever mischief may have followed from men's looking for nothing else but this facility of execution, and supposing that a picture was assuredly all right if only it were done with broad dashes of the brush, still the truth remains the same: – that because it is not intended that men shall torment or weary themselves with any earthly labor, it is appointed that the noblest results should only be attainable by a certain ease and decision of manipulation. I only wish people understood this much of sculpture, as well as of painting, and could see that the finely finished statue is, in ninety-nine cases out of a hundred, a far more vulgar work than that which shows rough signs of the right hand laid to the workman's hammer: but at all events, in painting it is felt by all men, and justly felt. The freedom of the lines of nature can only be represented by a similar freedom in the hand that follows them; there are curves in the flow of the hair, and in the form of the features, and in the muscular outline of the body, which can in no wise be caught but by a sympathetic freedom in the stroke of the pencil. I do not care what example is taken, be it the most subtle and careful work of Leonardo himself, there will be found a play and power and ease in the outlines, which no *slow* effort could ever imitate. And if the Pre-Raphaelites do not understand how this kind of power, in its highest perfection, may be united with the most severe rendering of all other orders of truth, and especially of those with which they themselves have most sympathy, let them look at the drawings of John Lewis.

These then are the principal lessons which we have to learn from Turner, in his second or central period of labor. There is one more, however, to be received; and that is a warning; for towards the close of it, what with doing small conventional vignettes for publishers, making showy drawings from sketches taken by other people of places he had never seen, and touching up the bad engravings from his works submitted to him almost every day, – engravings utterly destitute of animation, and which had to be raised into a specious brilliancy by scratching them over with white, spotty lights, he gradually got inured to many conventionalities, and even falsities; and, having trusted for ten or twelve years almost entirely to his memory and invention, living I believe mostly in London, and receiving a new sensation only from the burning of the Houses of Parliament, he painted many pictures between 1830 and 1840 altogether unworthy of him. But he was not thus to close his career.

In the summer either of 1840 or 1841, he undertook another journey into Switzerland. It was then at least forty years since he had first seen the Alps; (the source of the Arveron, in Mr. Fawkes's collection, which could not have been painted till he had seen the thing itself, bears date 1800,) and the direction of his journey in 1840 marks his fond memory of that earliest one; for, if we look over the Swiss studies and drawings executed in his first period, we shall be struck with his fondness for the pass of the St. Gothard; the most elaborate drawing in the Farnley collection is one of the Lake of Lucerne from Fluelen; and, counting the Liber Studiorum subjects, there are, to my knowledge, six compositions taken at the same period from the pass of St. Gothard, and, probably, several others are in existence. The valleys of Sallenche, and Chamouni, and Lake of Geneva, are the only other Swiss scenes which seem to have made very profound impressions on him.

He returned in 1841 to Lucerne; walked up Mont Pilate on foot, crossed the St. Gothard, and returned by Lausanne and Geneva. He made a large number of colored sketches on this journey, and realised several of them on his return. The drawings thus produced are different from all that had preceded them, and are the first which belong definitely to what I shall henceforth call his Third period.

The perfect repose of his youth had returned to his mind, while the faculties of imagination and execution appeared in renewed strength; all conventionality being done away with by the force of the impression which he had received from the Alps, after his long separation from them. The drawings are marked by a peculiar largeness and simplicity of thought: most of them by deep serenity, passing into melancholy; all by a richness of color, such as he had never before conceived. They, and the works done in following years, bear the same relation to those of the rest of his life that the colors of sunset do to those of the day; and will be recognised, in a few years more, as the noblest landscapes ever yet conceived by human intellect.

Such has been the career of the greatest painter of this century. Many a century may pass away before there rises such another; but what greatness any among us may be capable of, will, at least, be best attained by following in his path; by beginning in all quietness and hopefulness to use whatever powers we may possess to represent the things around us as we see and feel them; trusting to the close of life to give the perfect crown to the course of its labors, and knowing assuredly that the determination of the degree in which watchfulness is to be exalted into invention, rests with a higher will than our own. And, if not greatness, at least a certain good, is thus to be achieved; for though I have above spoken of the mission of the more humble artist, as if it were merely to be subservient to that of the antiquarian or the man of science, there is an ulterior aspect in which it is not subservient, but superior. Every archæologist, every natural philosopher, knows that there is a peculiar rigidity of mind brought on by long devotion to logical and analytical inquiries. Weak men, giving themselves to such studies, are utterly hardened by them, and become incapable of understanding anything nobler, or even of feeling the value of the results to which they lead. But even the best men are in a sort injured by them, and pay a definite price, as in most other matters, for definite advantages. They gain a peculiar strength, but lose in tenderness, elasticity, and impressibility. The man who has gone, hammer in hand, over the surface of a romantic country, feels no longer, in the mountain ranges he has so laboriously explored, the sublimity or mystery with which they were veiled when he first beheld them, and with which they are adorned in the mind of the passing traveller. In his more informed conception, they arrange themselves like a dissected model: where another man would be awe-struck by the magnificence of the precipice, he sees nothing but the emergence of a fossiliferous rock, familiarised already to his imagination as extending in a shallow stratum, over a perhaps uninteresting district; where the unlearned spectator would be touched with strong emotion by the aspect of the snowy summits which rise in the distance, he sees only the culminating points of a metamorphic formation, with an uncomfortable web of fan-like fissures radiating, in his imagination, through their centres[8]. That in the grasp he has obtained of the inner relations of all these things to the universe, and to man, that in the views which have been opened to him of natural energies such as no human mind would have ventured to conceive, and of past states of being, each in some new way bearing witness to the unity of purpose and everlastingly consistent providence of the Maker of all things, he has received reward well worthy the sacrifice, I would not for an instant deny; but the sense of the loss is not less painful to him if his mind be rightly constituted; and it would be with infinite gratitude that he would regard the man, who, retaining in his delineation of natural scenery a fidelity to the facts of science so rigid as to make his work at once acceptable and credible to the most sternly critical intellect, should yet invest its features again with the sweet veil of their daily aspect; should make them dazzling with the splendor of wandering light, and involve them in the unsearchableness of stormy obscurity; should restore to the divided anatomy its visible vitality of operation, clothe naked crags with soft forests, enrich the mountain ruins with bright pastures, and lead the thoughts from the monotonous recurrence of the phenomena of the physical world, to the sweet interests and sorrows of human life and death.

FOOTNOTES

1. It was not a little curious, that in the very number of the Art Union which repeated this direct falsehood about the Pre-Raphaelite rejection of "linear perspective" (by-the-bye, the next time J. B. takes upon him to speak of any one connected with the Universities, he may as well first ascertain the difference between a Graduate and an Under-Graduate), the second plate given should have been of a picture of Bonington's, – a professional landscape painter, observe, – for the want of *aërial* perspective in which the Art Union itself was obliged to apologise, and in which the artist has committed nearly as many blunders in *linear* perspective as there are lines in the picture.

2. These false statements may be reduced to three principal heads, and directly contradicted in succession.
The first, the current fallacy of society as well as of the press, was, that the Pre-Raphaelites imitated the *errors* of early painters.
A falsehood of this kind could not have obtained credence anywhere but in England, few English people, comparatively, having ever seen a picture of early Italian Masters. If they had, they would have known that the Pre-Raphaelite pictures are just as superior to the early Italian in skill of manipulation, power of drawing, and knowledge of effect, as inferior to them in grace of design; and that in a word, there is not a shadow of resemblance between the two styles. The Pre-Raphaelites imitate no pictures: they paint from nature only. But they have opposed themselves as a body to that kind of teaching above described, which only began after Raphael's time: and they have opposed themselves as sternly to the entire feeling of the Renaissance schools; a feeling compounded of indolence, infidelity, sensuality, and shallow pride. Therefore they have called themselves Pre-Raphaelites. If they adhere to their principles, and paint nature as it is around them, with the help of modern science, with the earnestness of the men

of the thirteenth and fourteenth centuries, they will, as I said, found a new and noble school in England. If their sympathies with the early artists lead them into mediævalism or Romanism, they will of course come to nothing. But I believe there is no danger of this, at least for the strongest among them. There may be some weak ones, whom the Tractarian heresies may touch; but if so, they will drop off like decayed branches from a strong stem. I hope all things from the school.

The second falsehood was, that the Pre-Raphaelites did not draw well. This was asserted, and could have been asserted only by persons who had never looked at the pictures.

The third falsehood was, that they had no system of light and shade. To which it may be simply replied that their system of light and shade is exactly the same as the Sun's; which is, I believe, likely to outlast that of the Renaissance, however brilliant.

3. He did not use his full signature, J. M. W., until about the year 1800.

4. I shall give a *catalogue raisonnée* of all this in the third volume of "Modern Painters."

5. The plate was, however, never published.

6. And the more probably because Turner was never fond of staying long at any place, and was least of all likely to make a pause of two or three days at the beginning of his journey.

7. Vide Modern Painters, Part II. Sect. III. Chap. IV. § 14.

8. This state of mind appears to have been the only one which Wordsworth had been able to discern in men of science; and in disdain of which, he wrote that short-sighted passage in the Excursion, Book III. l. 165-190, which is, I think, the only one in the whole range of his works which his true friends would have desired to see blotted out. What else has been found fault with as feeble or superfluous, is not so in the intense distinctive relief which it gives to his character. But these lines are written in mere ignorance of the matter they treat; in mere want of sympathy with the men they describe; for, observe, though the passage is put into the mouth of the Solitary, it is fully confirmed, and even rendered more scornful, by the speech which follows.

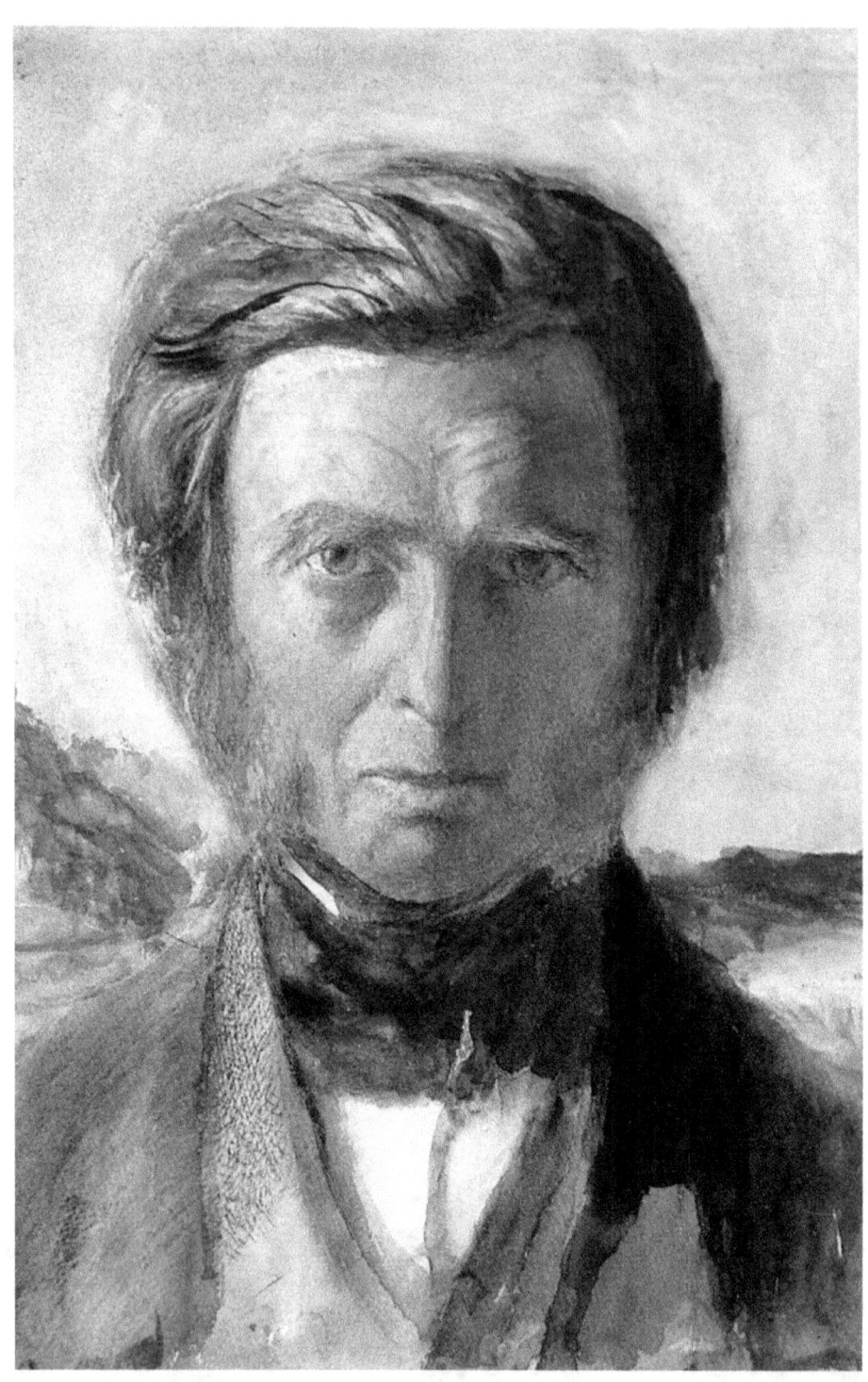

John Ruskin, Self-Portrait, 1875

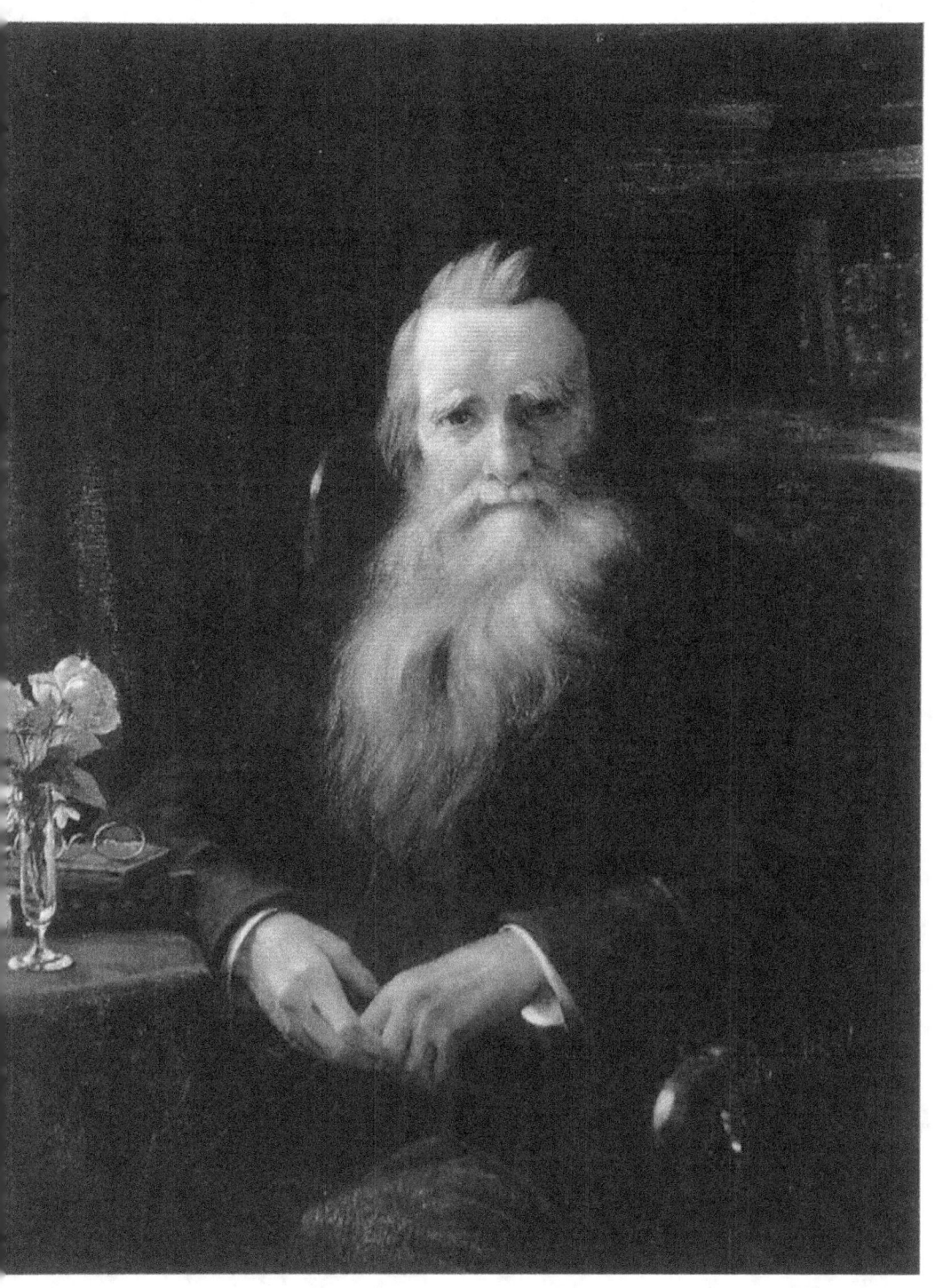

W.G. Collingwood,John Ruskin, 1897

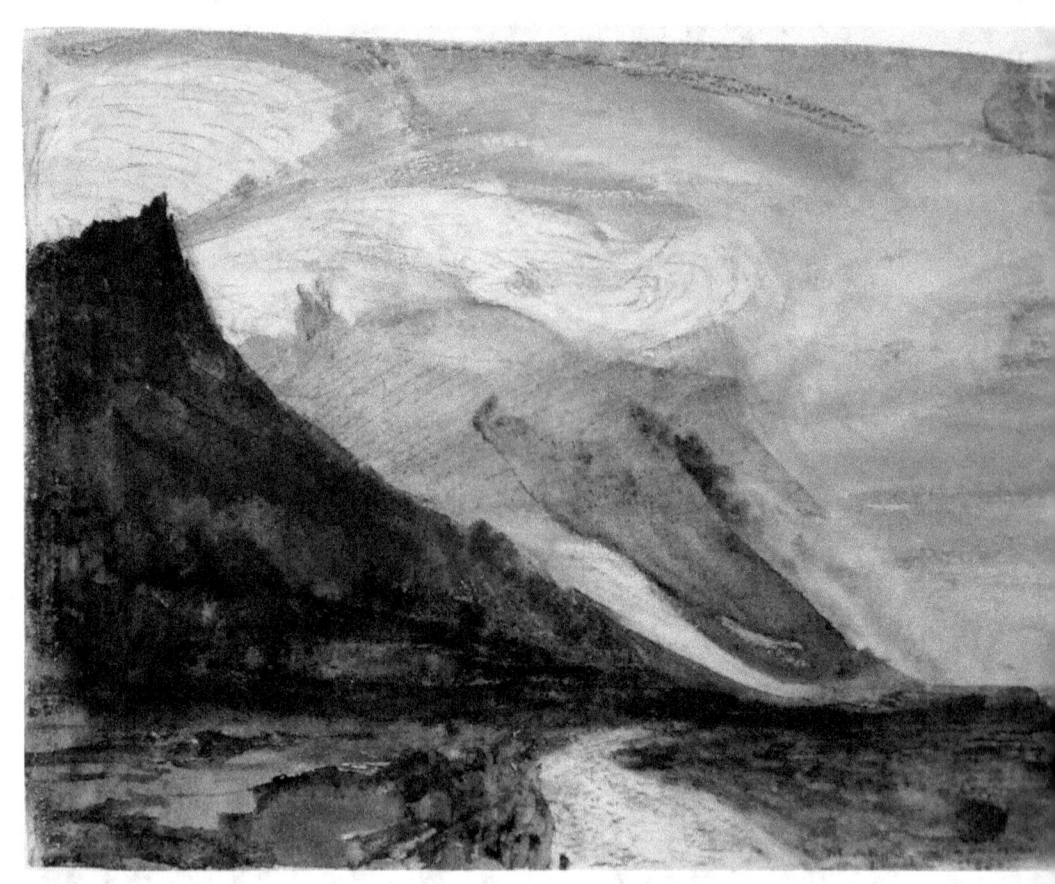

John Ruskin, Moonlight, Chamonix, 1888

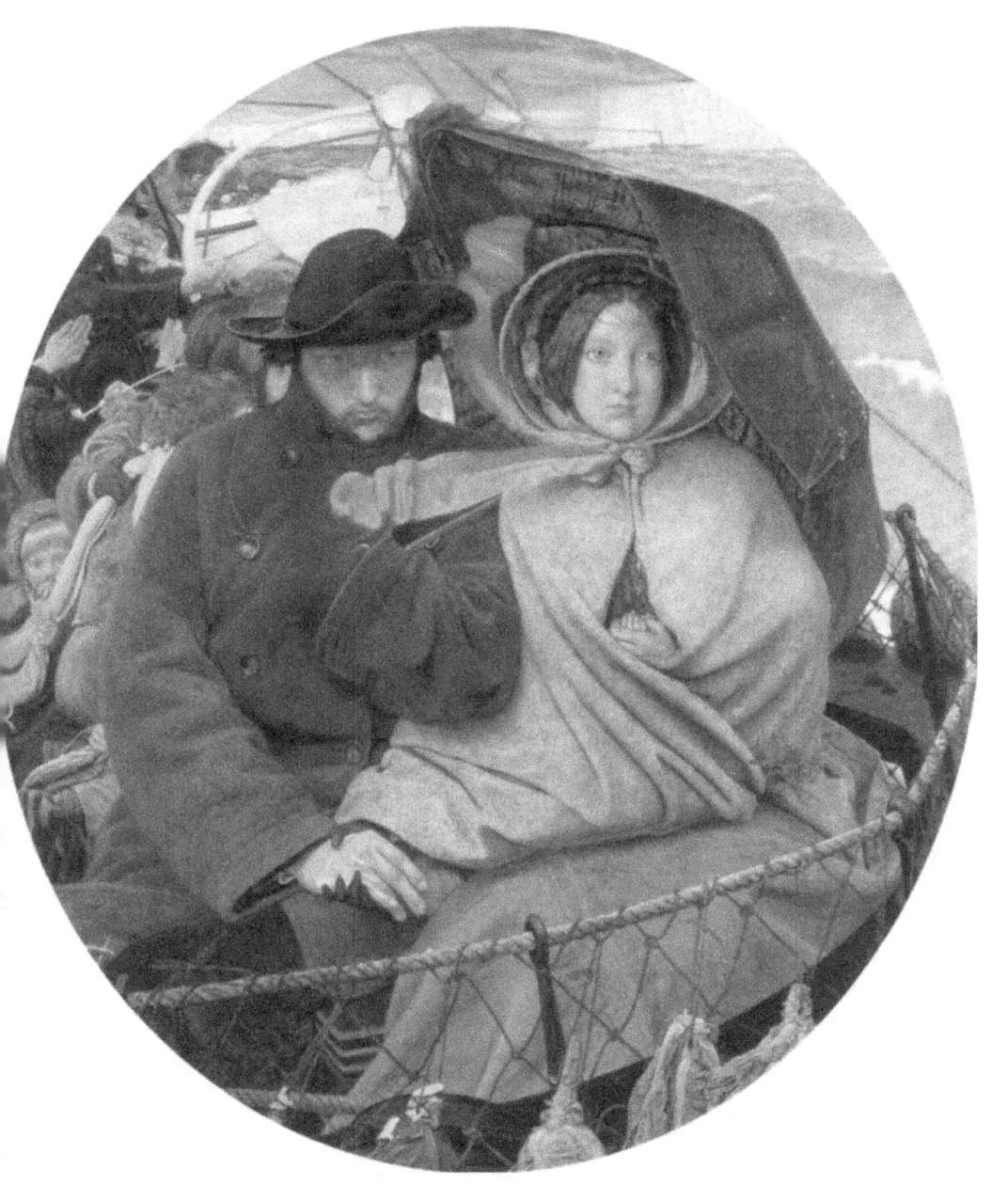

Ford Madox Brown, The Last of England, 1855,
Birmingham

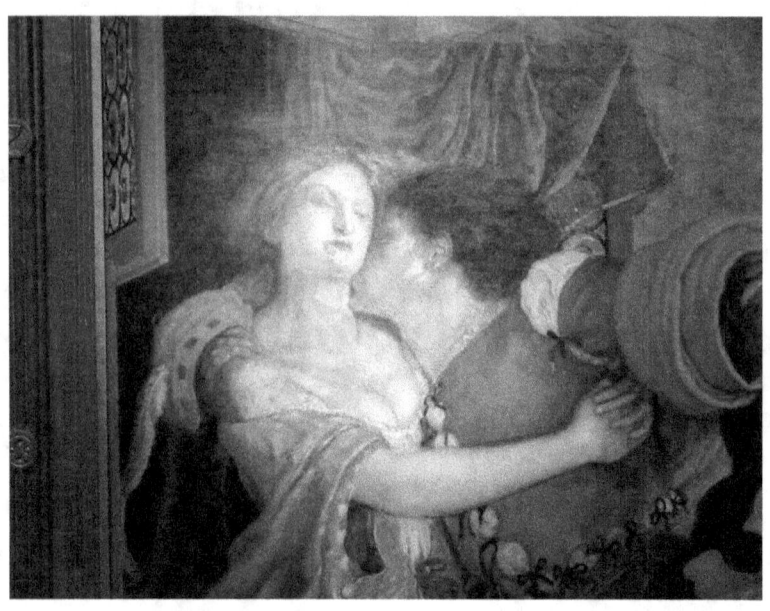

Ford Madox Brown, Romeo and Juliet, 1869-70, Delaware

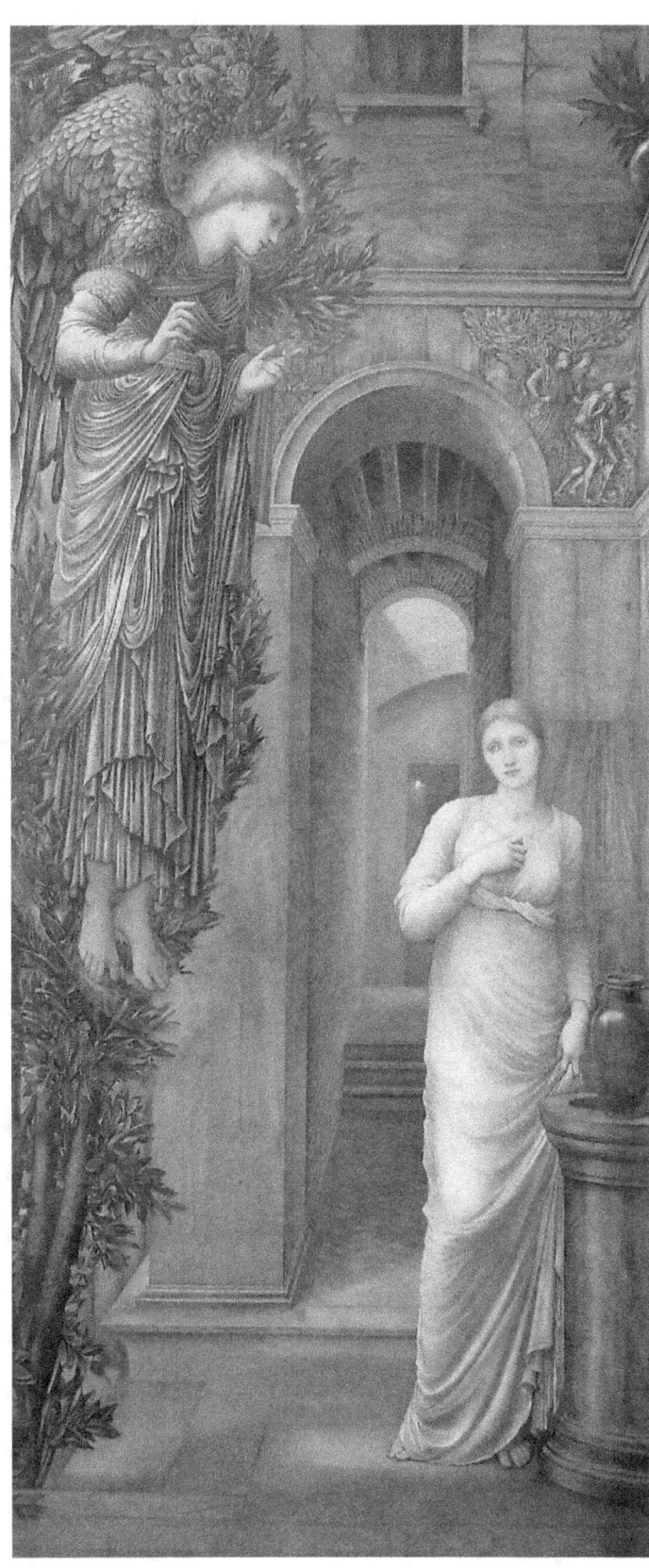

Edward Burne-Jones,
Annunciation, 1879

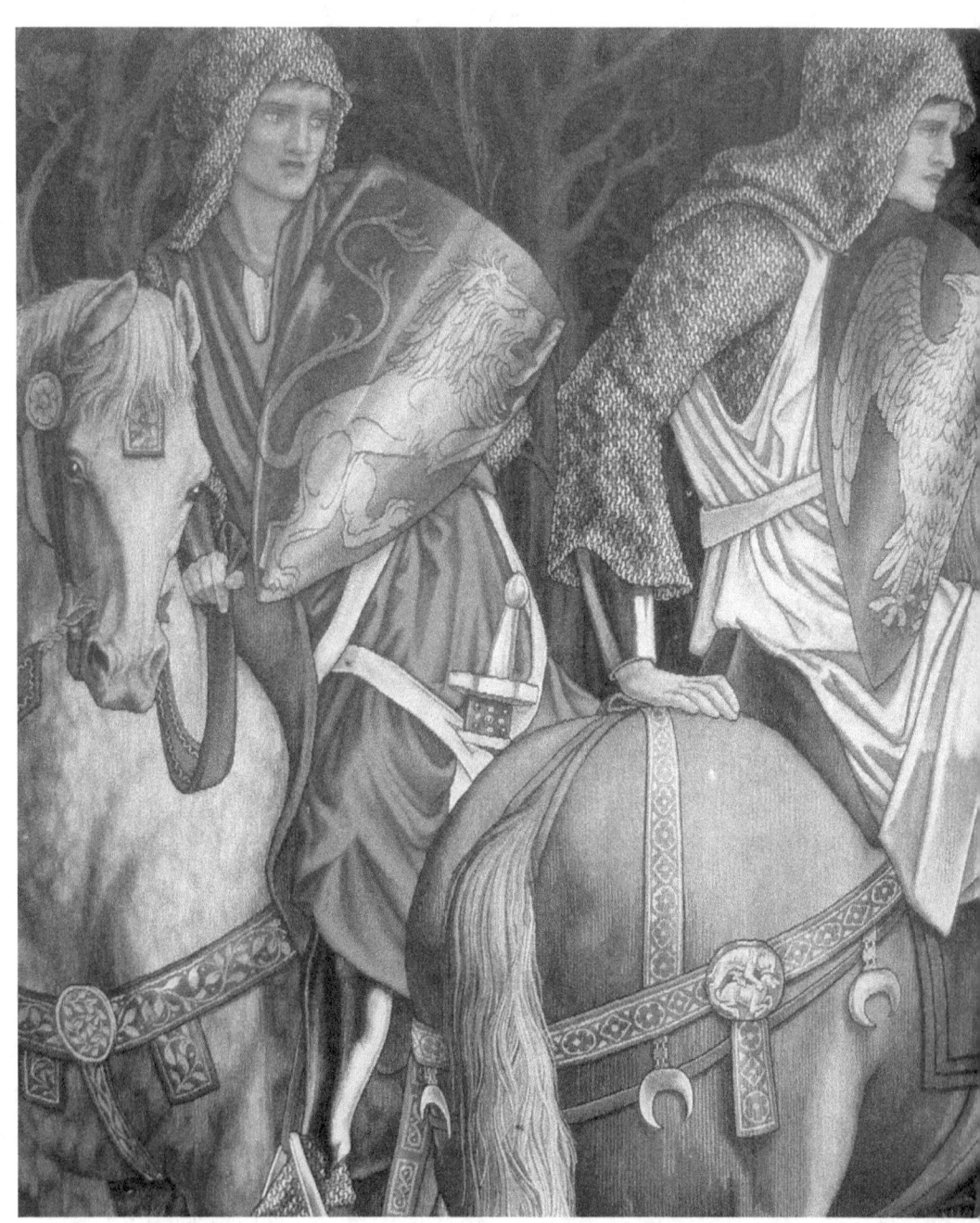

Edward Burne-Jones, The Fall of Lucifer, 1894, detail

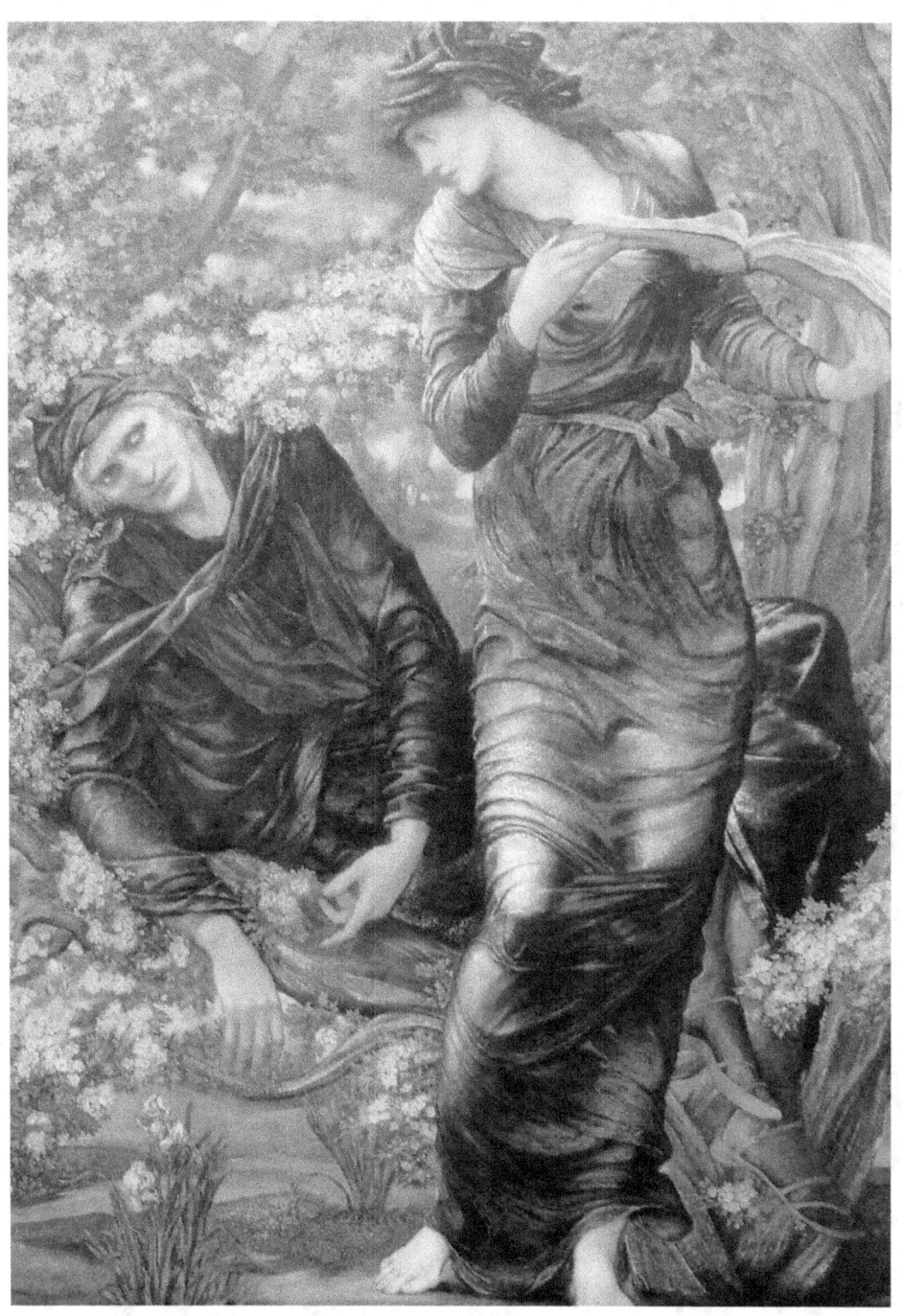

Edward Burne-Jones, The Beguiling of Merlin, 1874

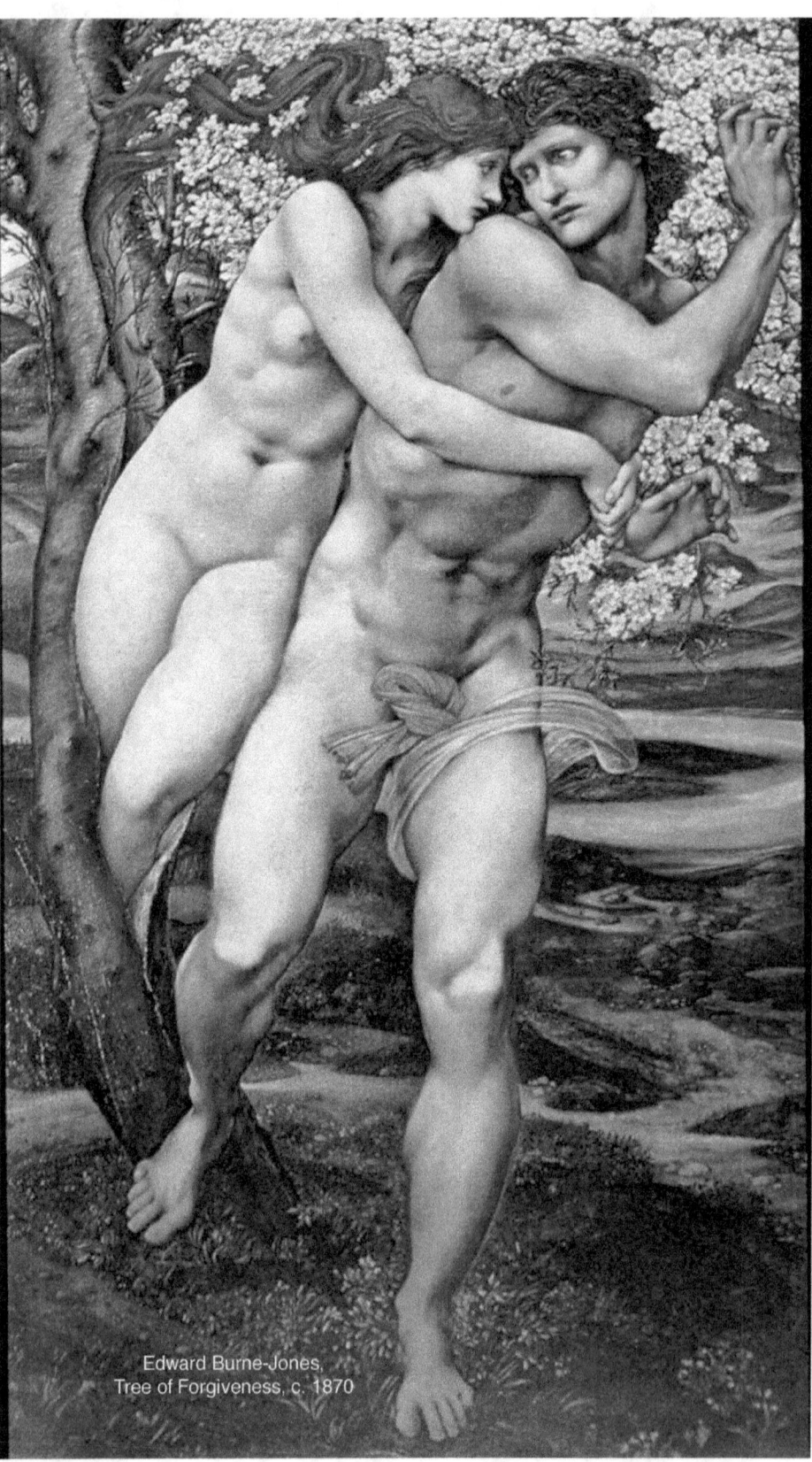

Edward Burne-Jones,
Tree of Forgiveness, c. 1870

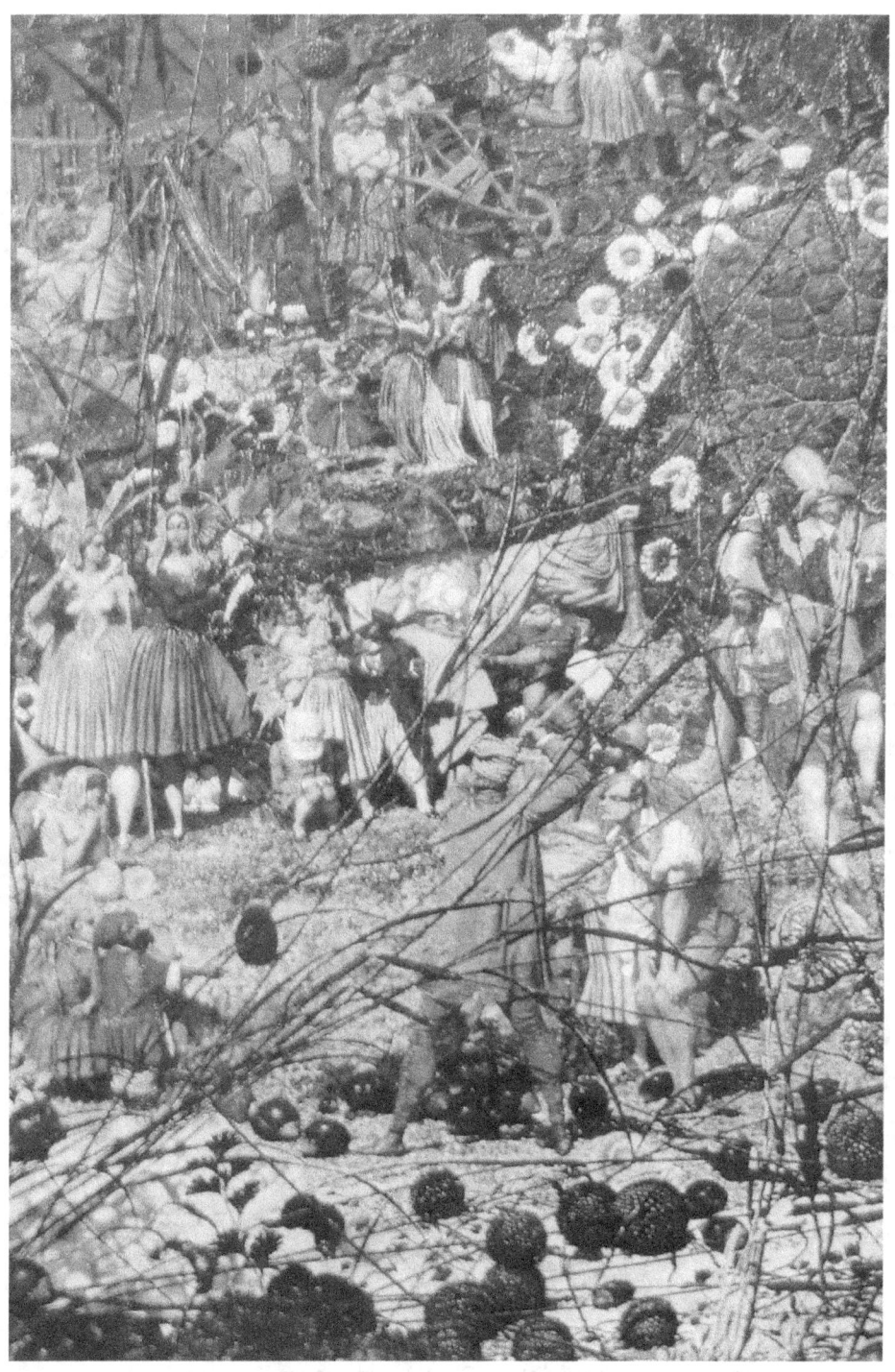

Richard Dadd, The Fairy-Feller's Master-Stroke, Tate, London

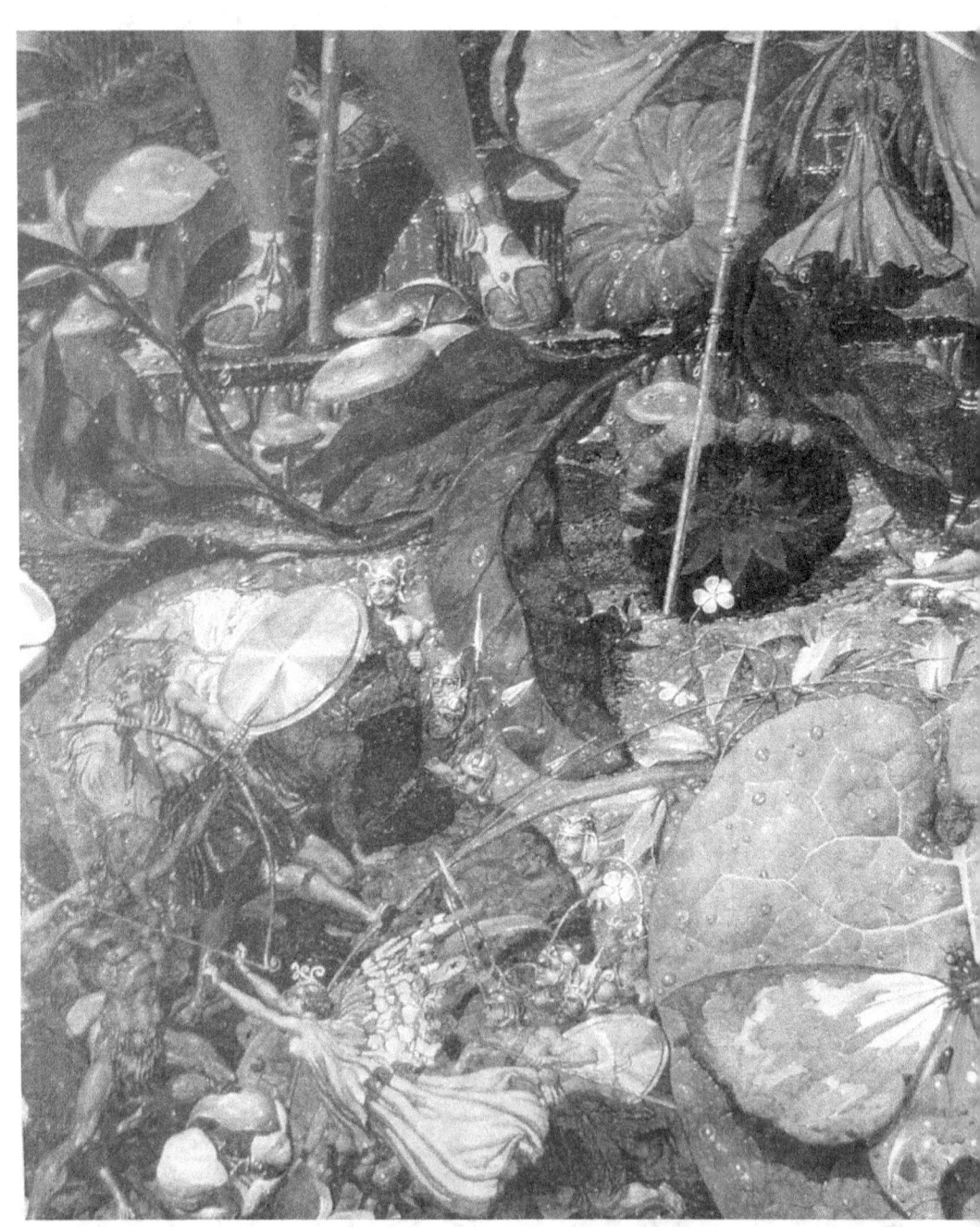

Richard Dadd, Contradiction: Oberon and Titania, 1854/ 58, detail

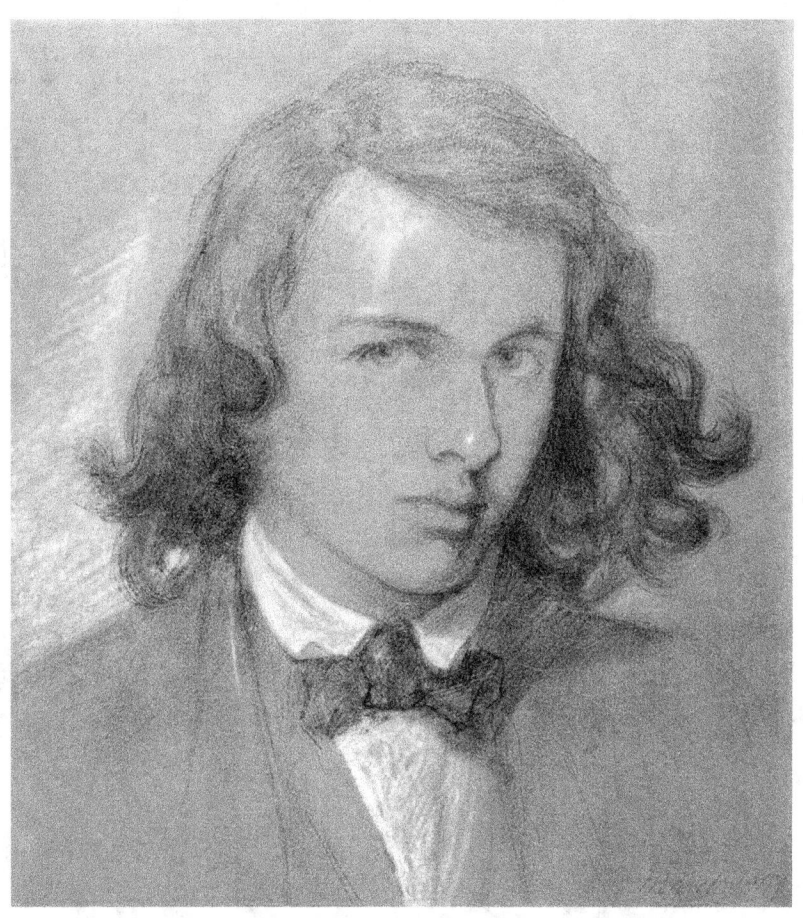

Dante Gabriel Rossetti, Self-Portrait, 1847,
National Portrait Gallery, London

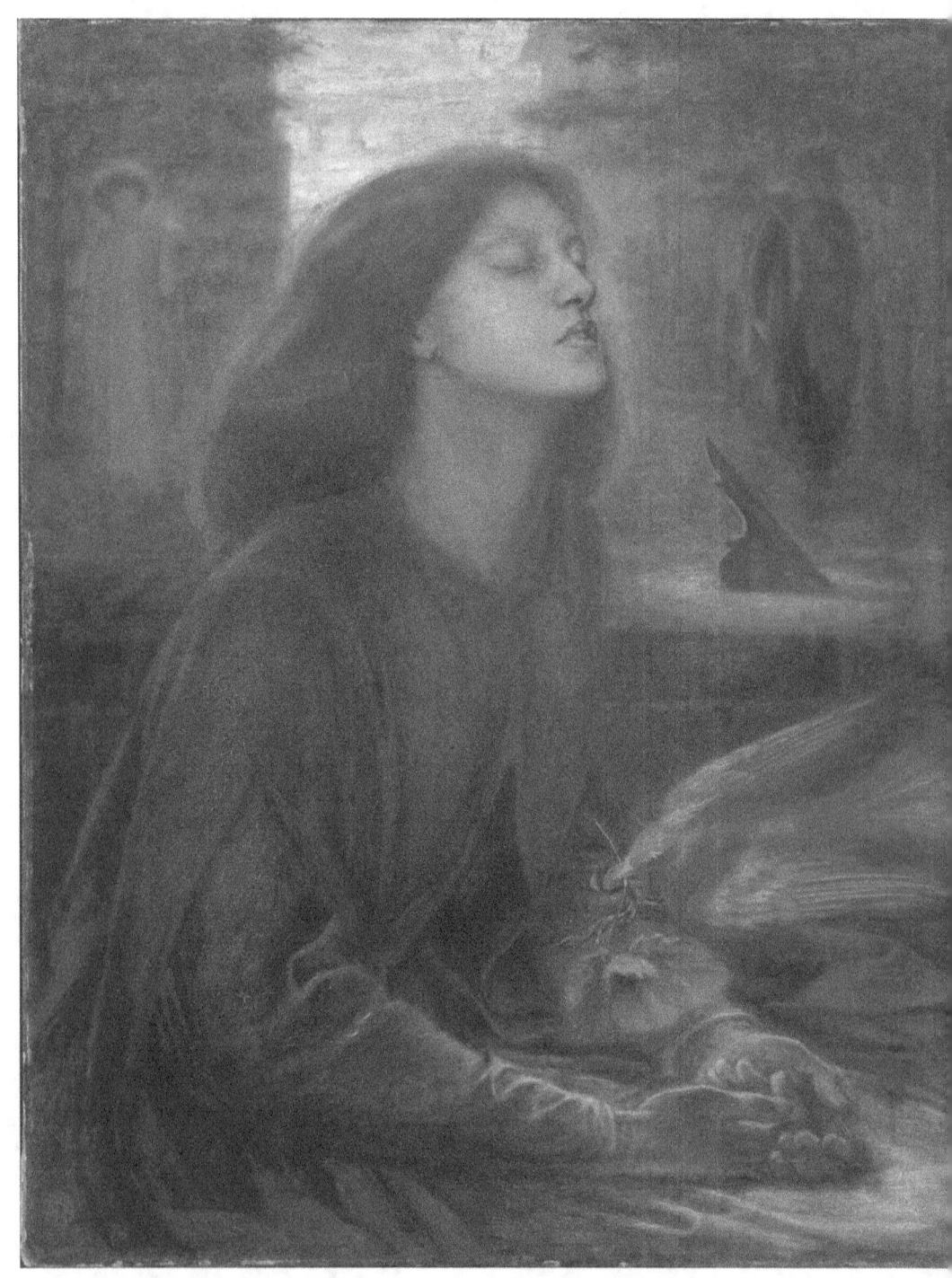

Dante Gabriel Rossetti, Beata Beatrix, 1864-70, Tate Britain

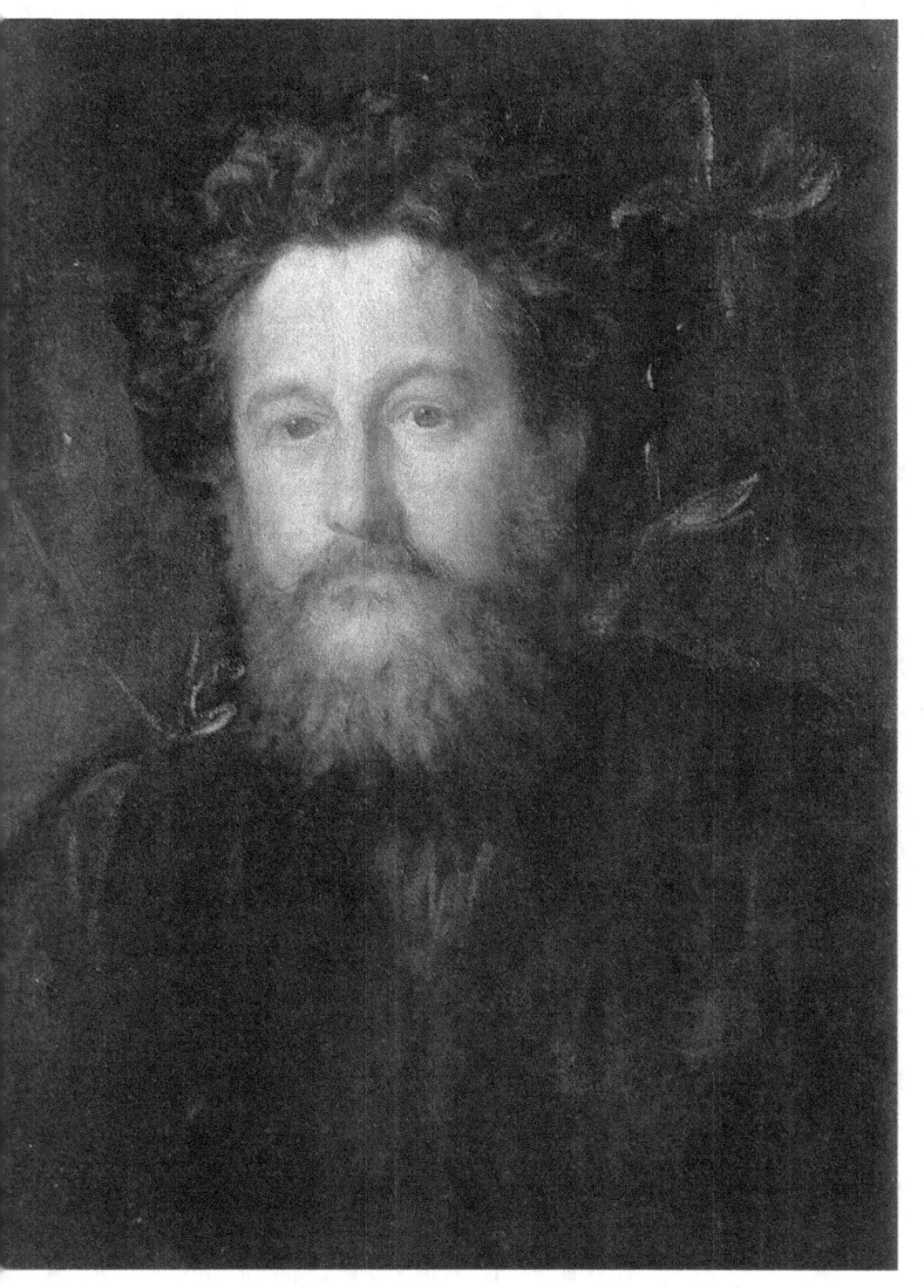

George Frederic Watts, Portrait of William Morris, 1870

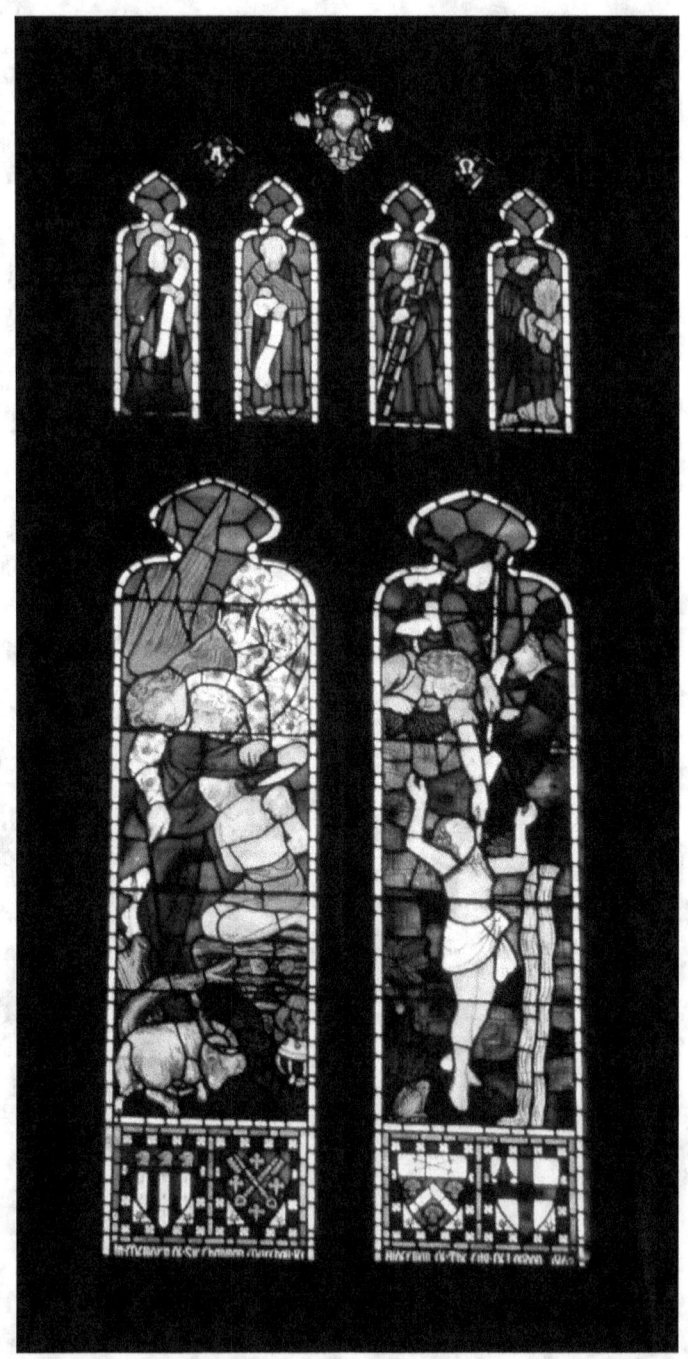

William Morris, Glass, Peterborough Cathedral, 1870

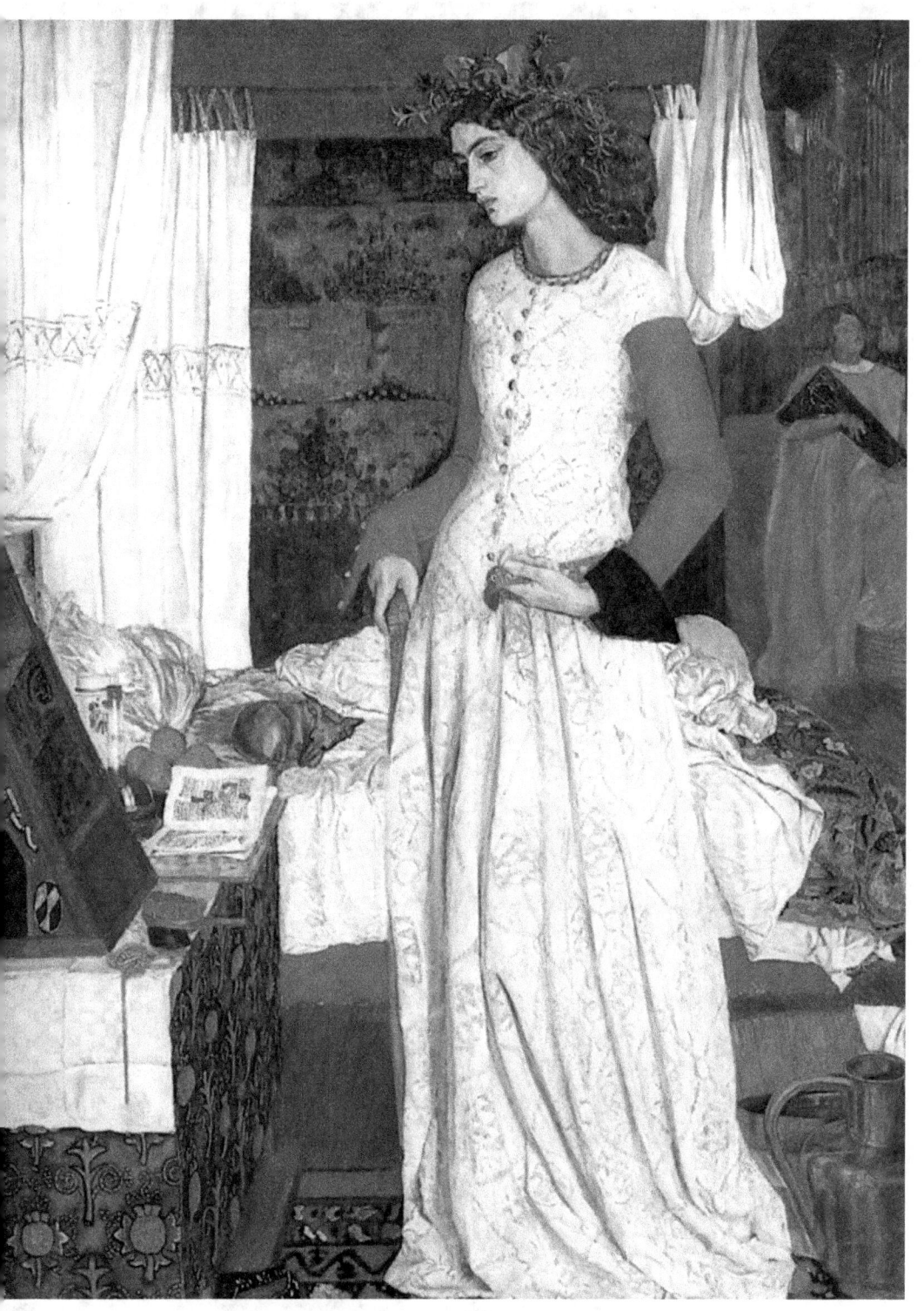

William Morris, La Belle Iseult, 1858, Tate Gallery

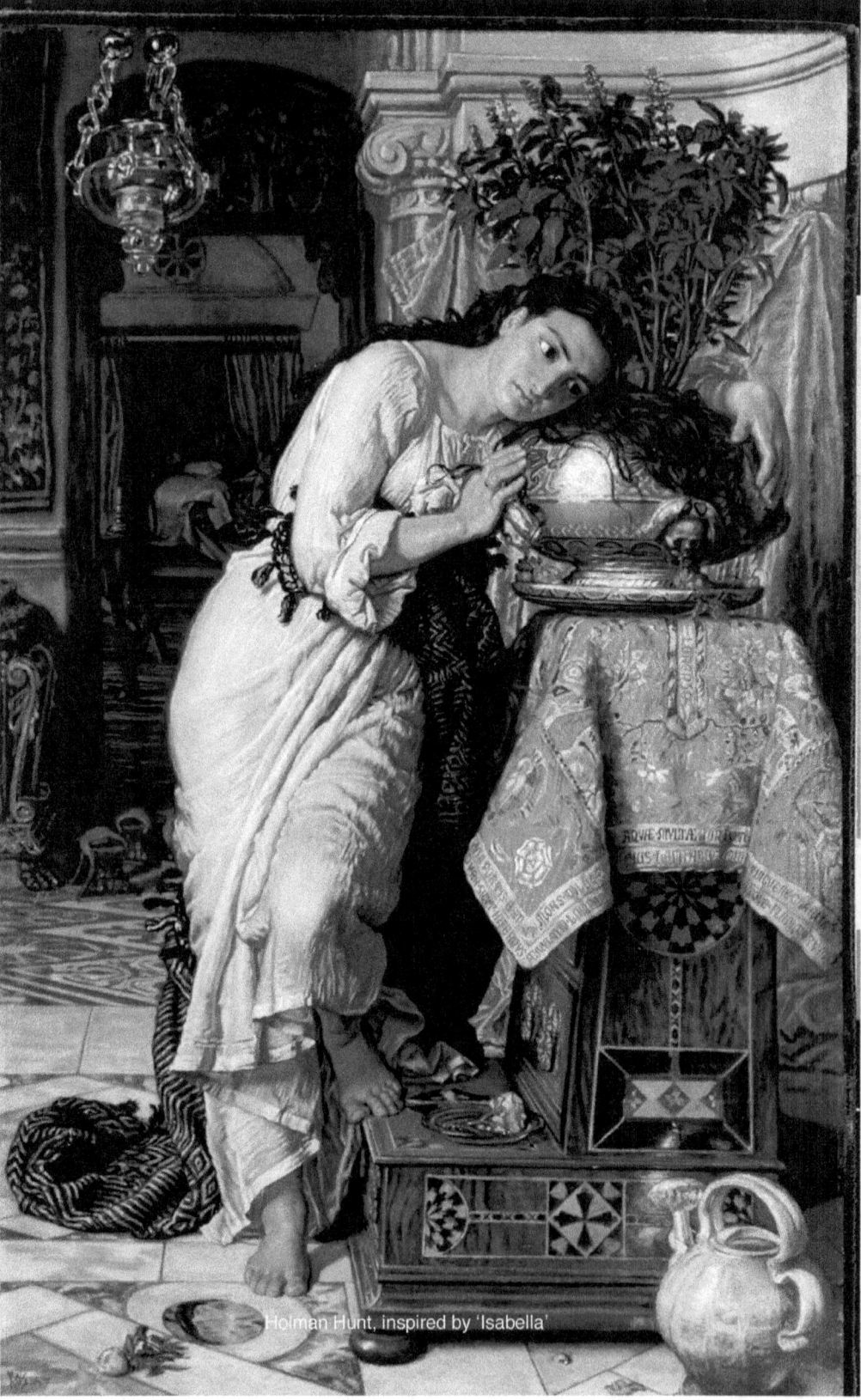

Holman Hunt, inspired by 'Isabella'

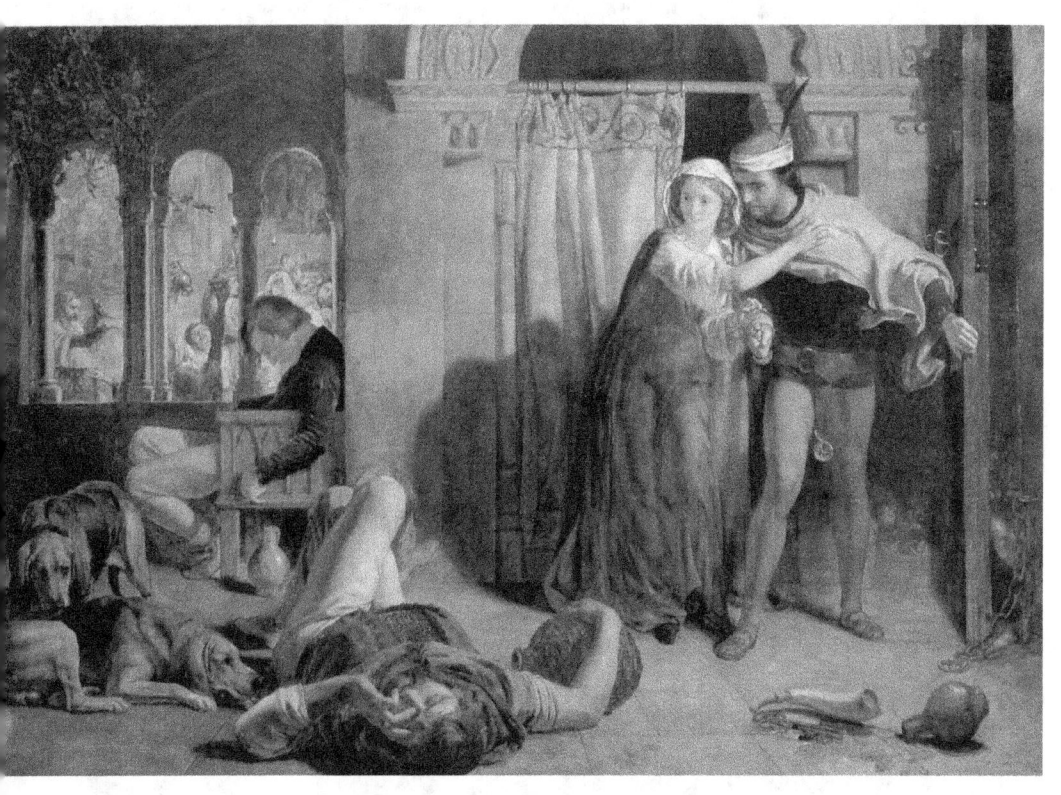

John William Holman Hunt, The Flight of Madeline and Porphyro

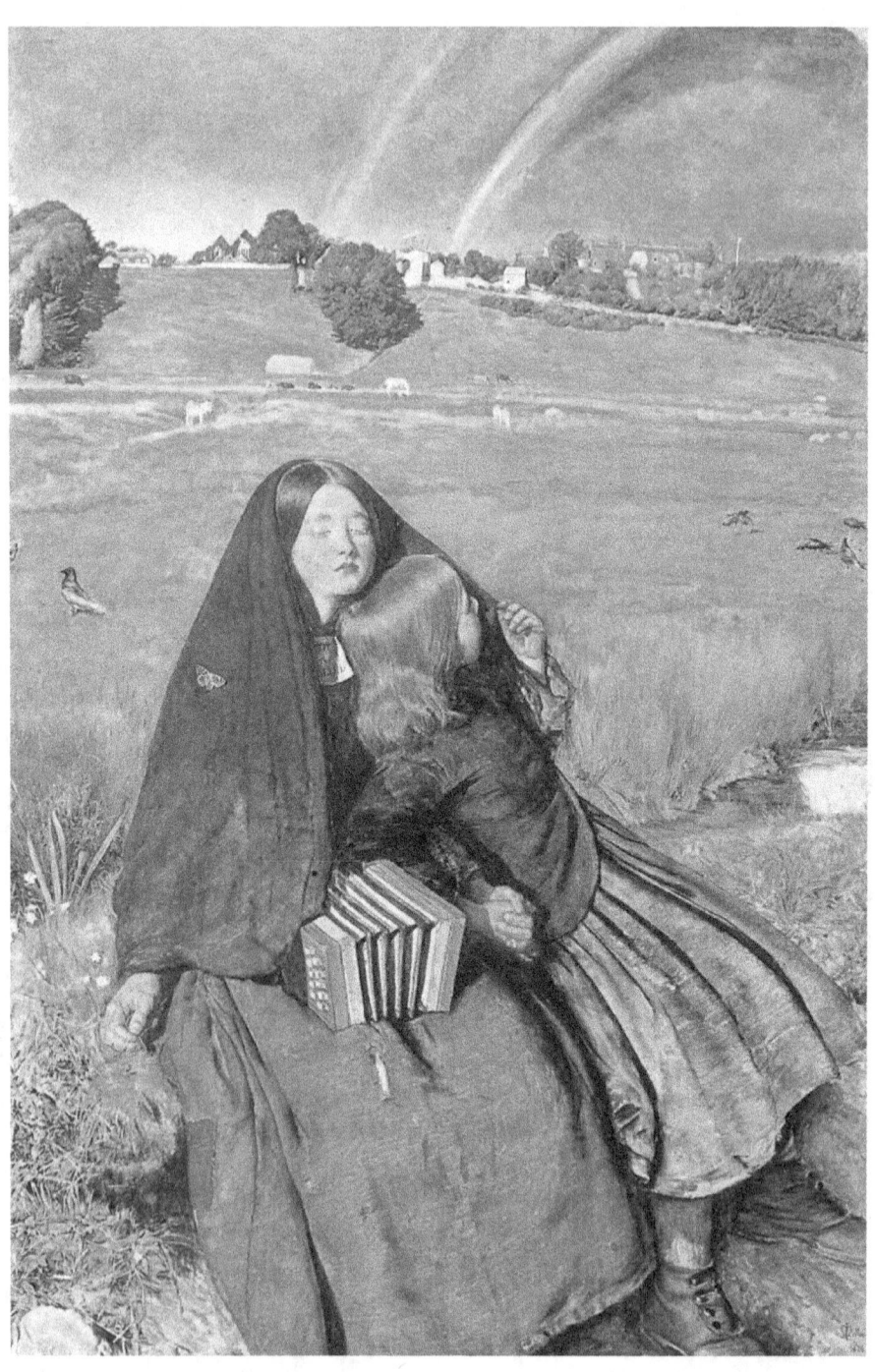

John Everett Millais, Blind Girl, 1885, Birmingham

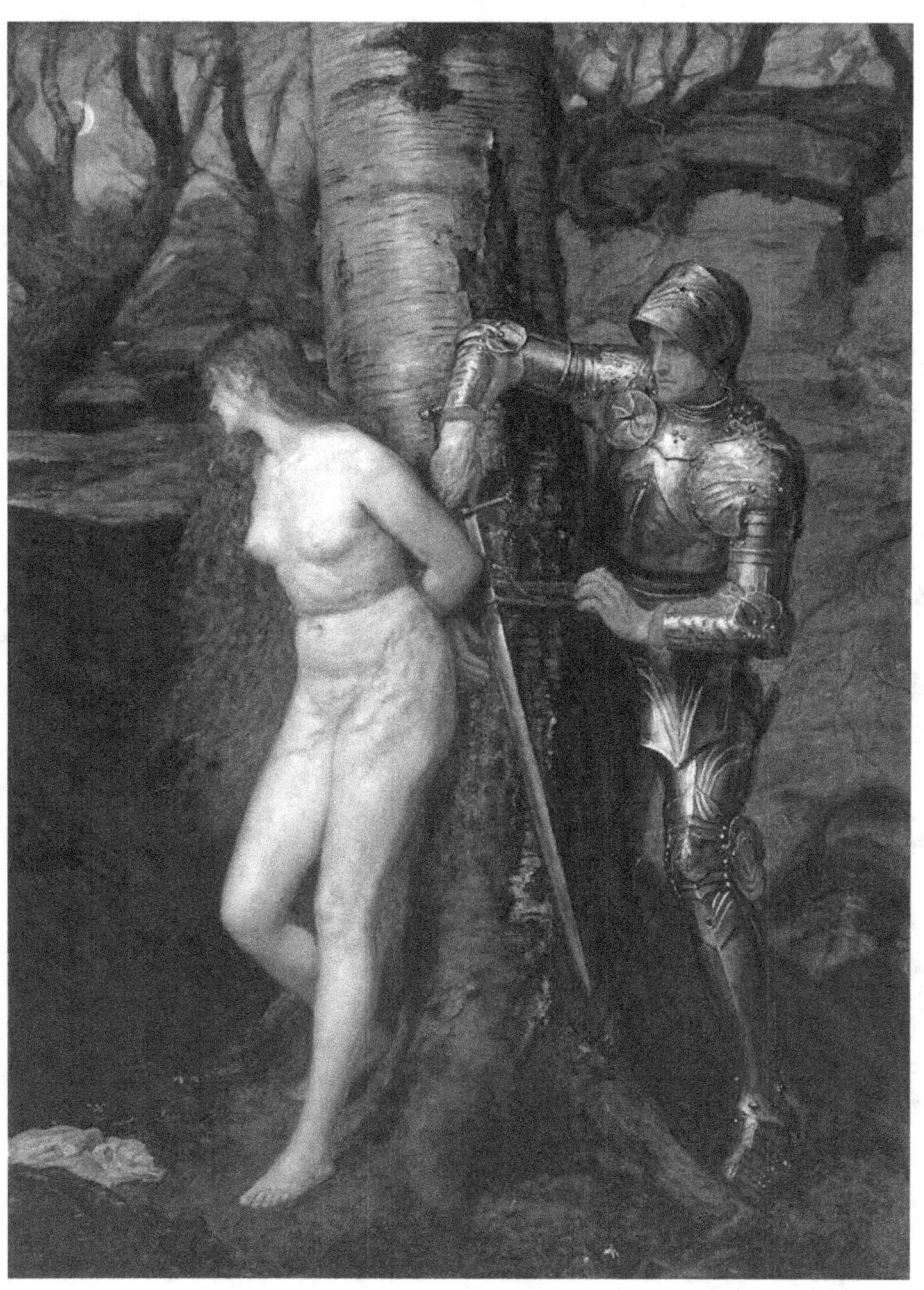

John Everett Millais, The Knight Errant, 1870, Tate, London

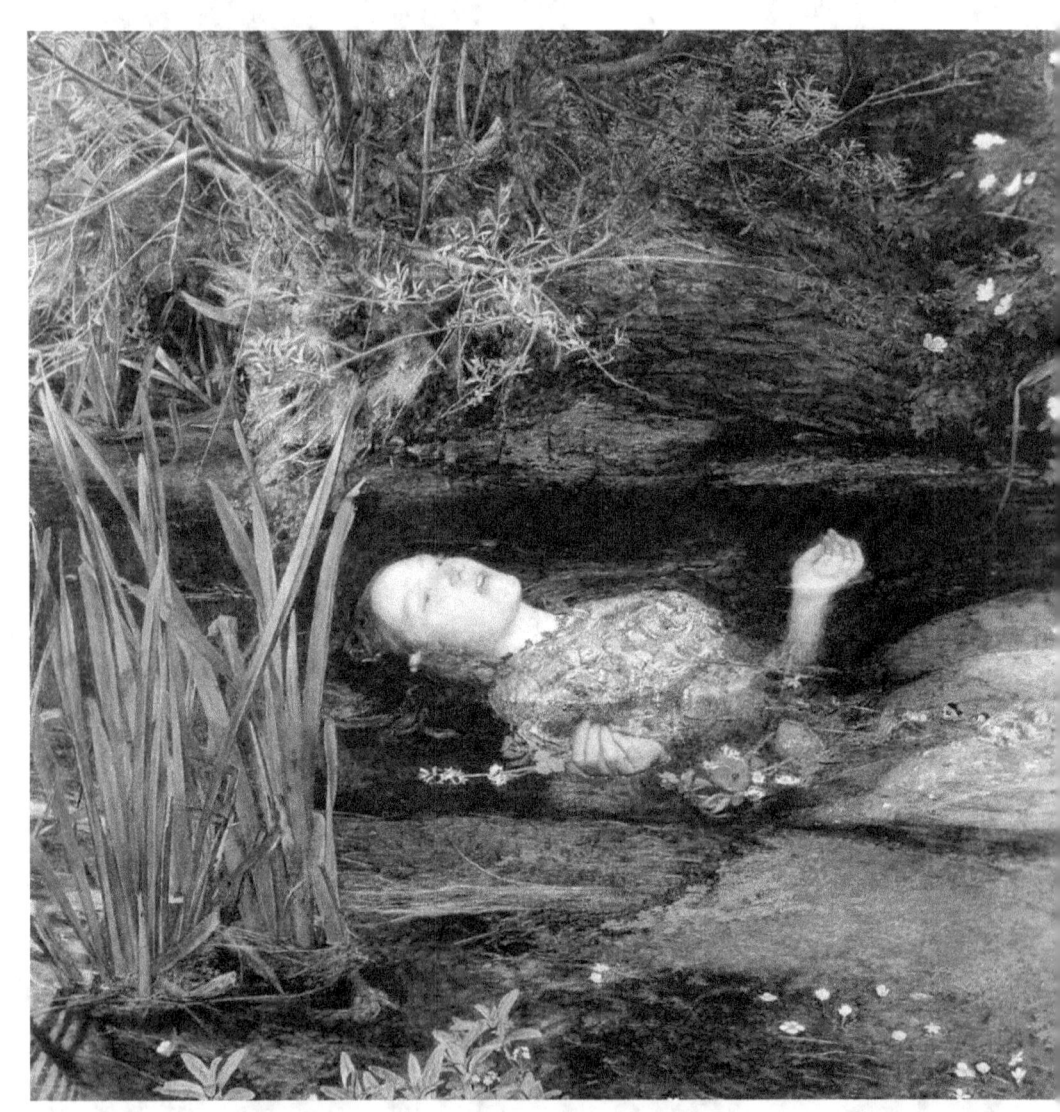

John Everett Millais, Ophelia.

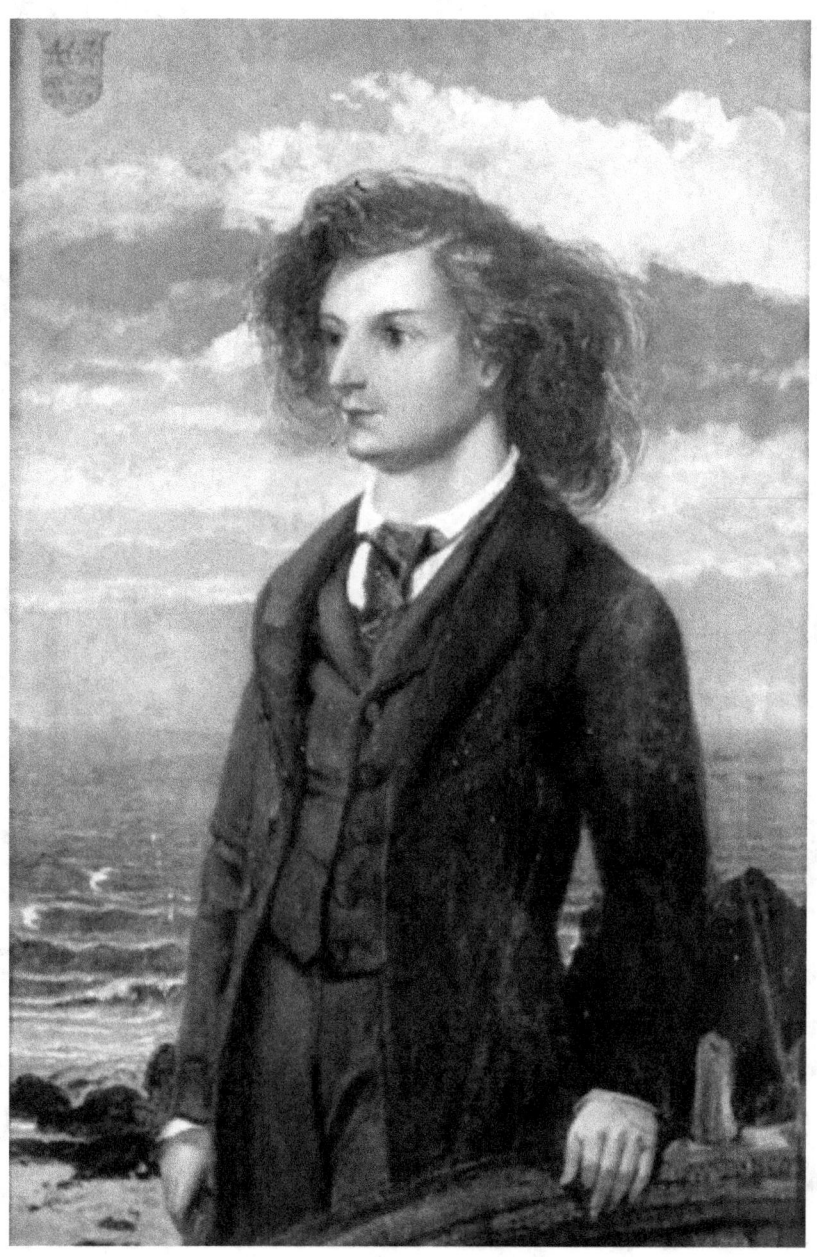

William Bell Scott, Algernon Charles Swinburne, Baillol College

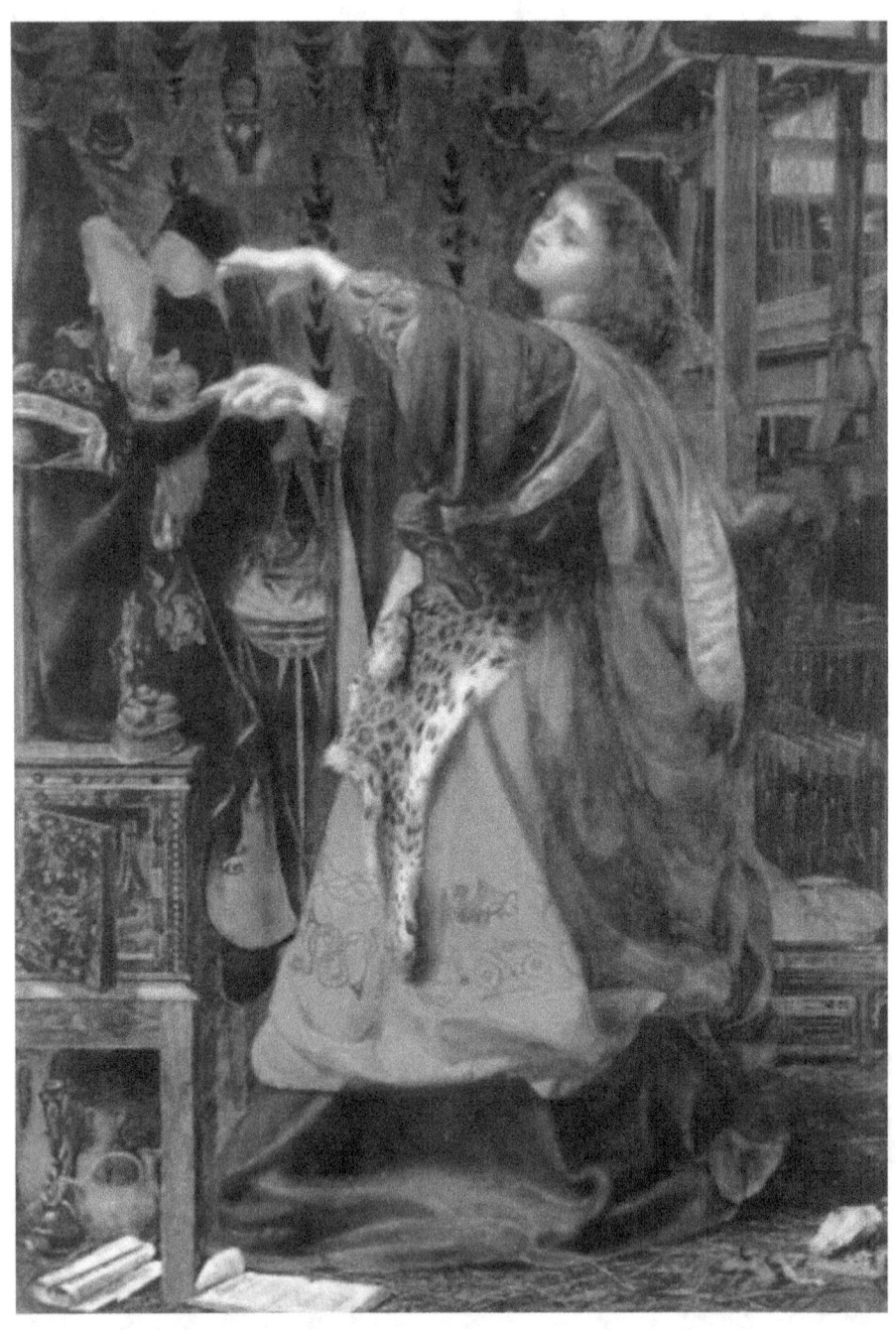

Frederick Sandys, Morgan le Fay, 1863-34, Birmingham

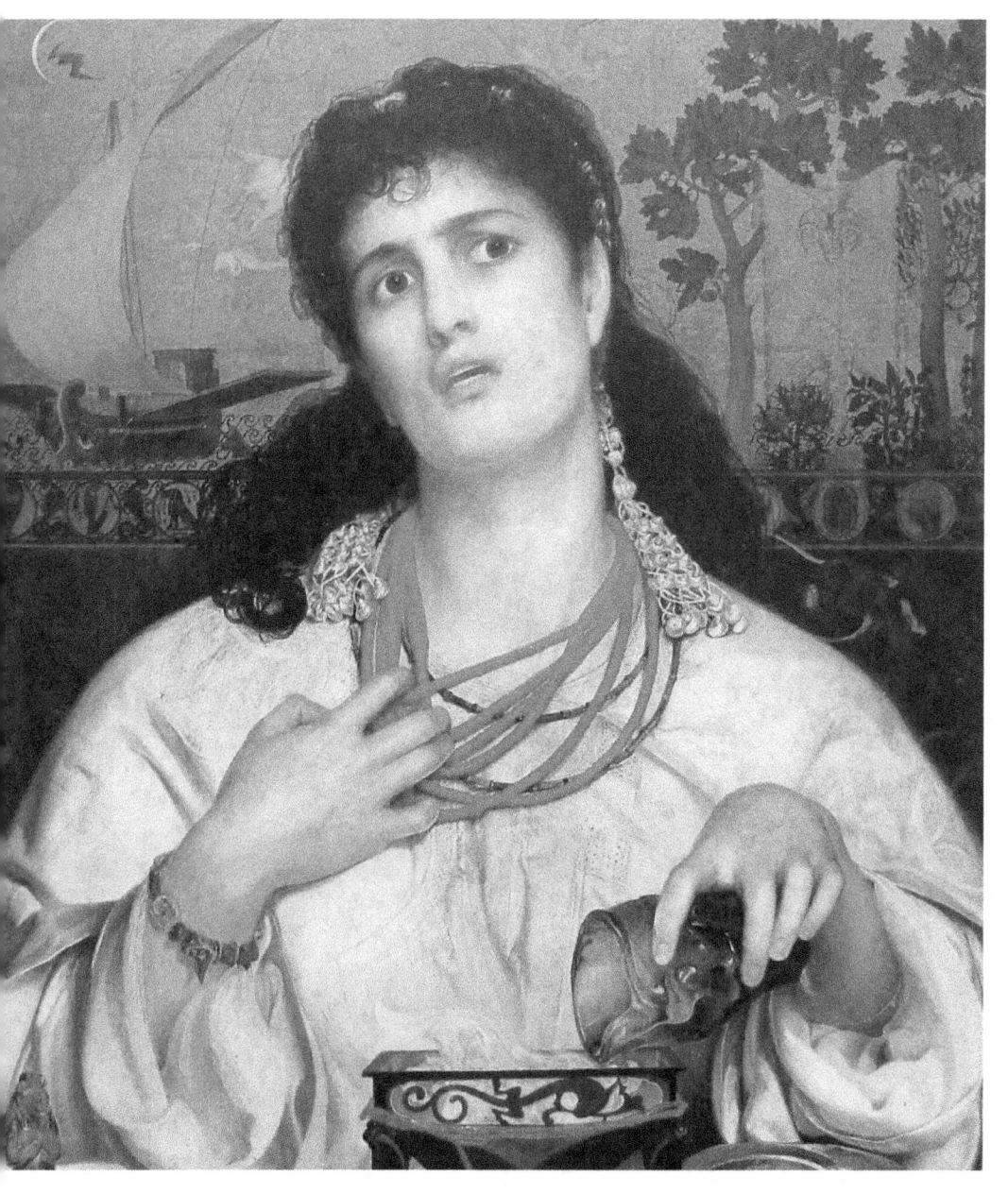

Frederick Sandys, Medea, 1868

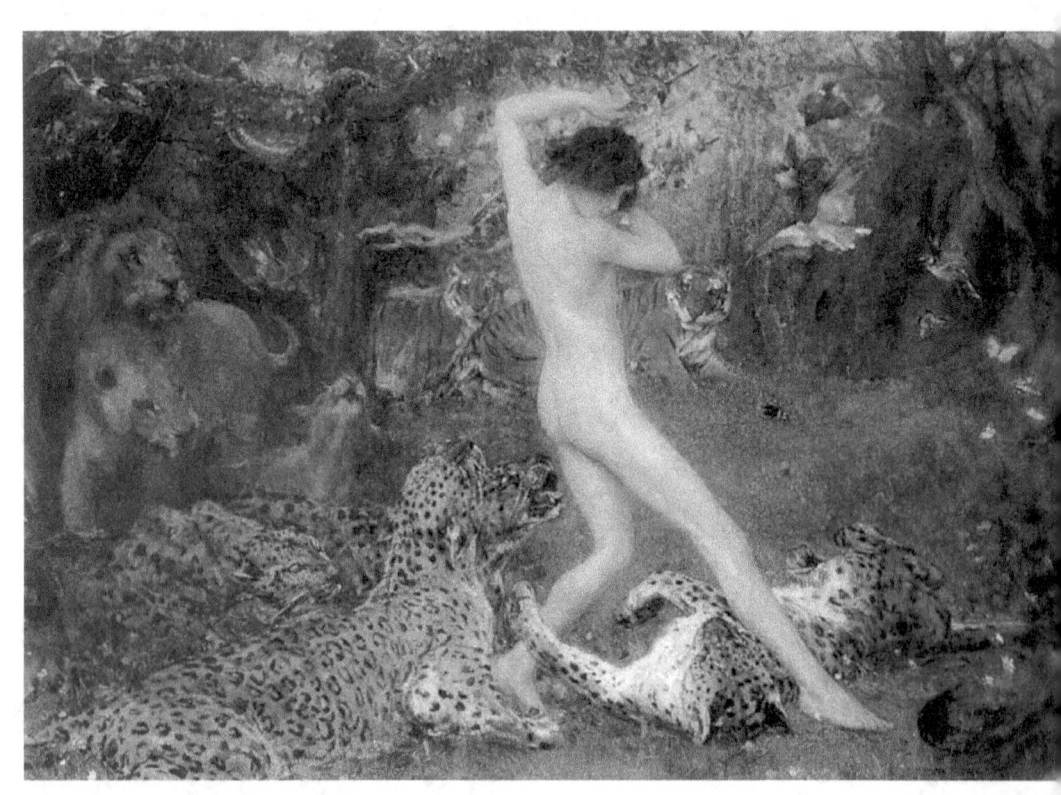

John Macallan Swan, Orpheus, 1896

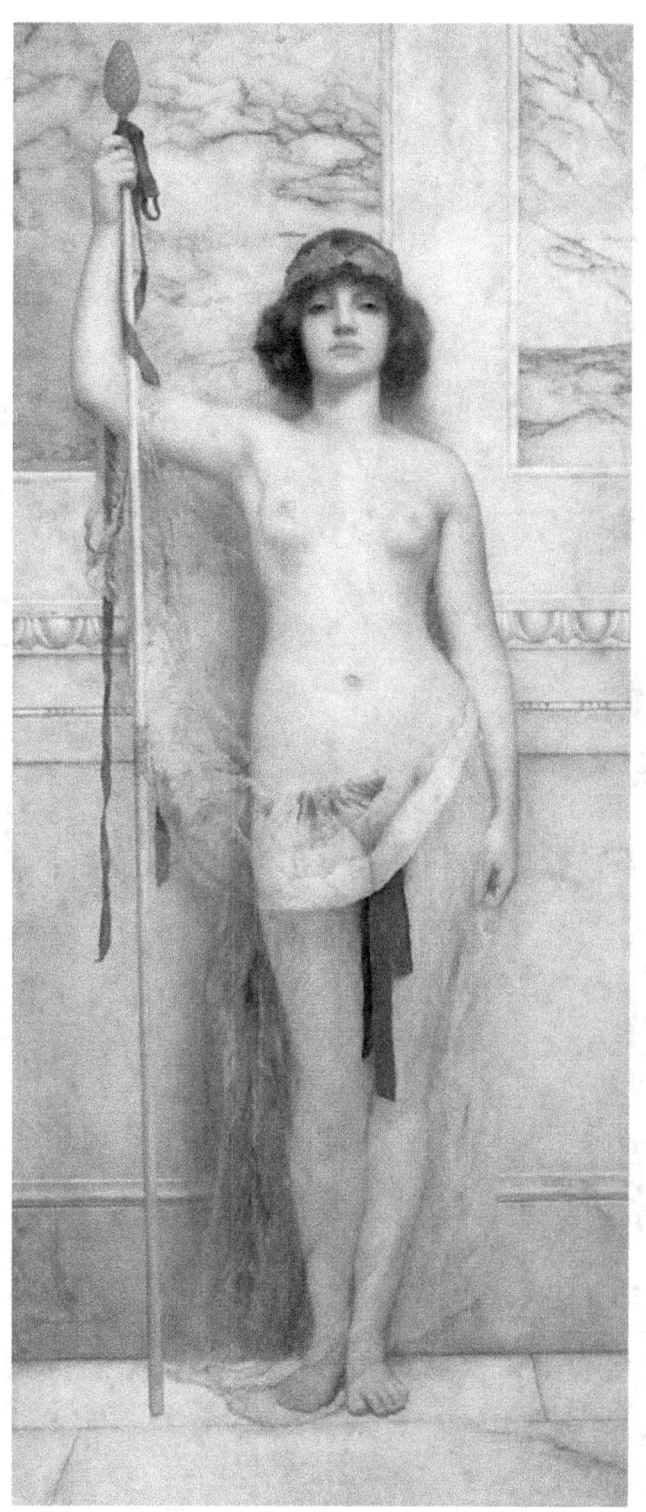

John Godward, A Priestess, 1893

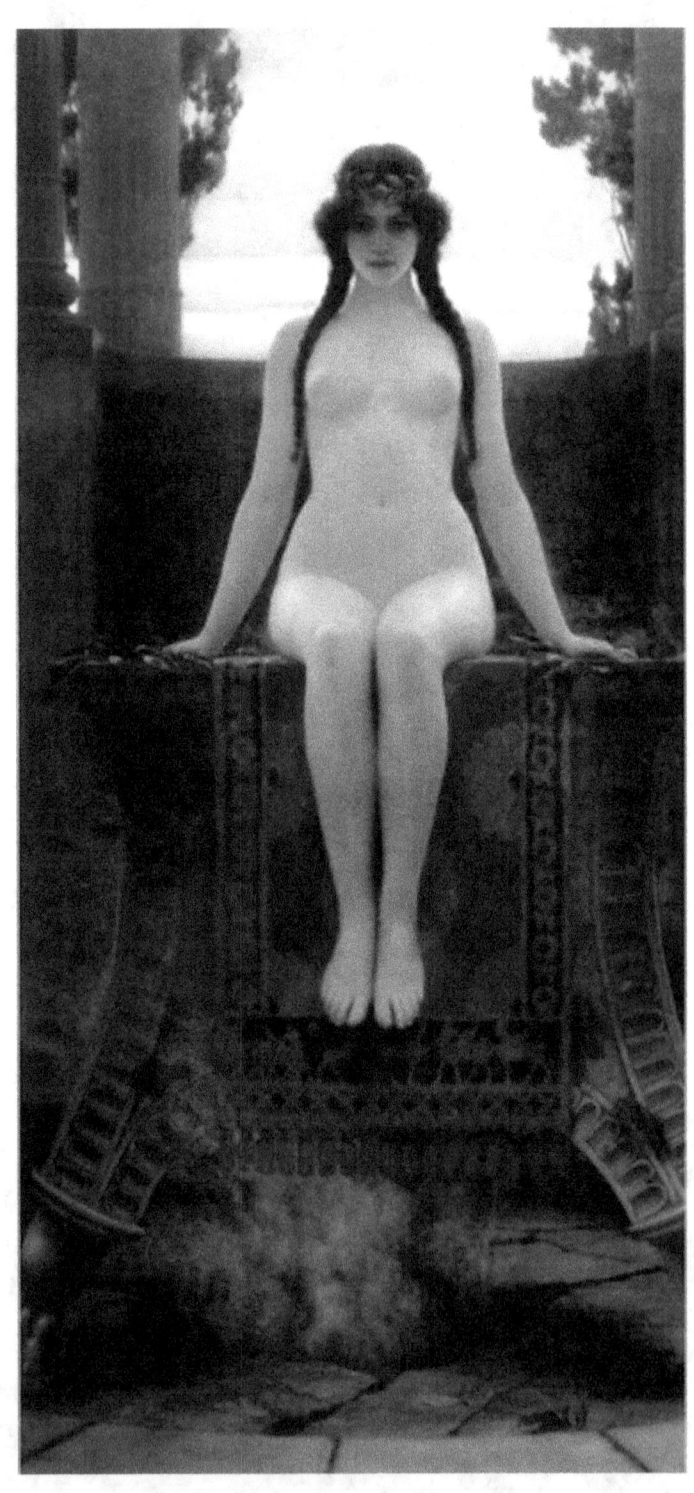

John Godward, The Delphic Oracle, 1899

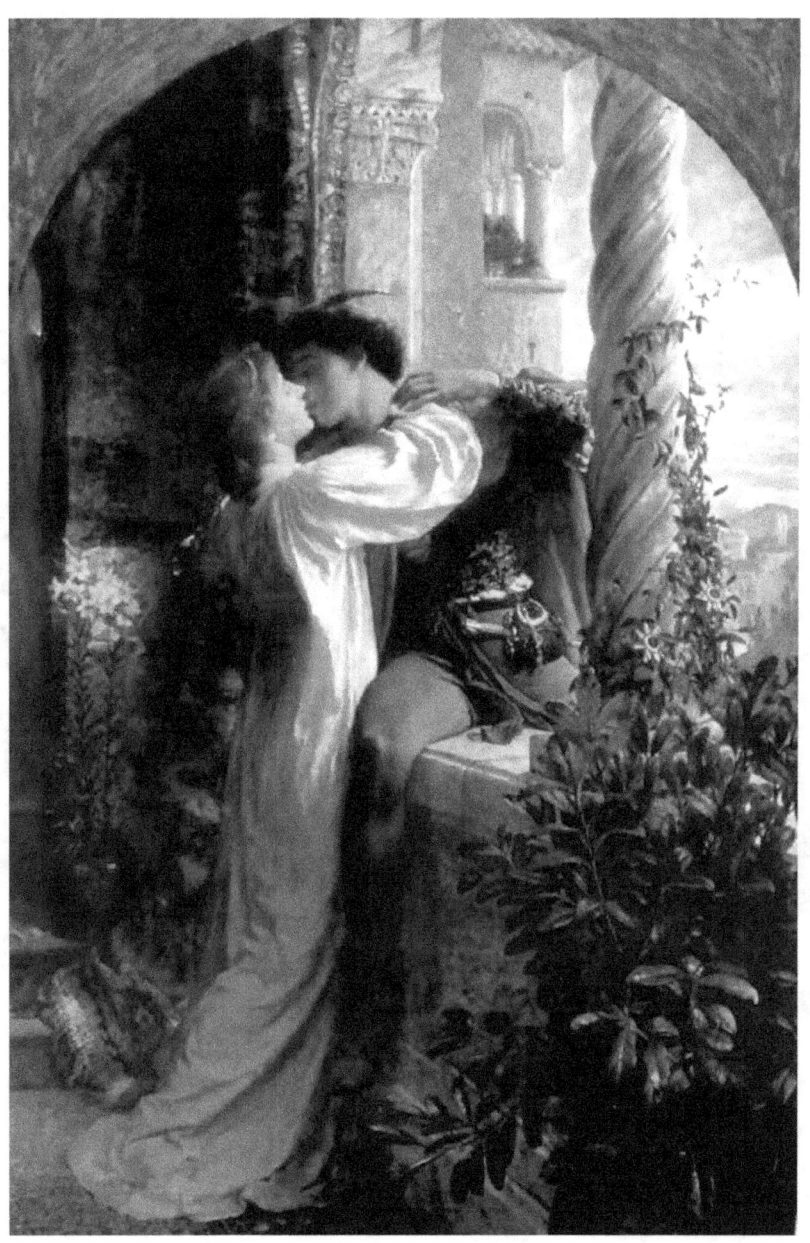

Francis Dicksee, Romeo & Juliet, 1884, Southampton

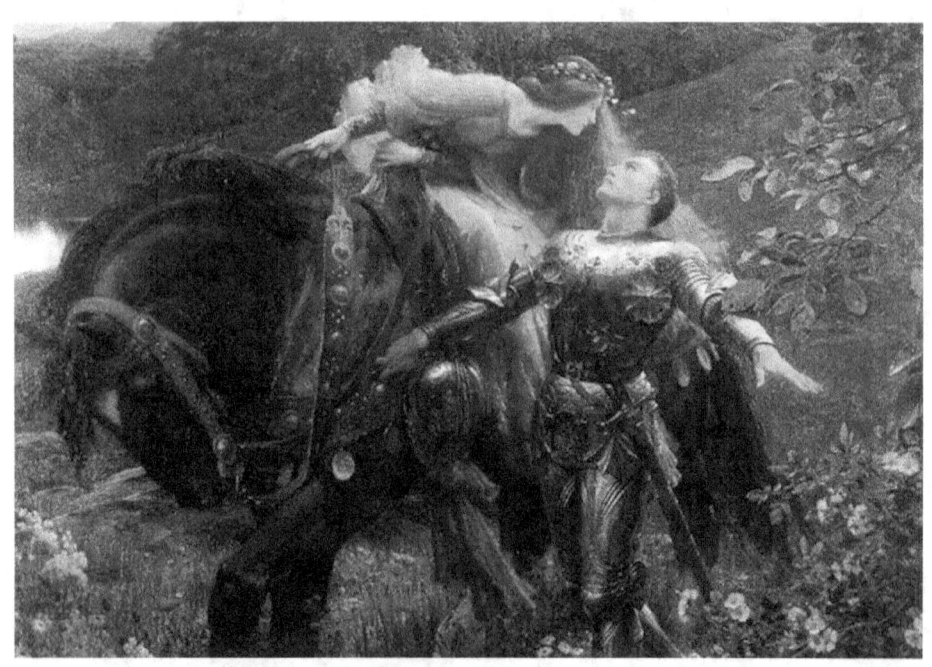

Sir Francis Dicksee, 'La Belle Dame Sans Merci'

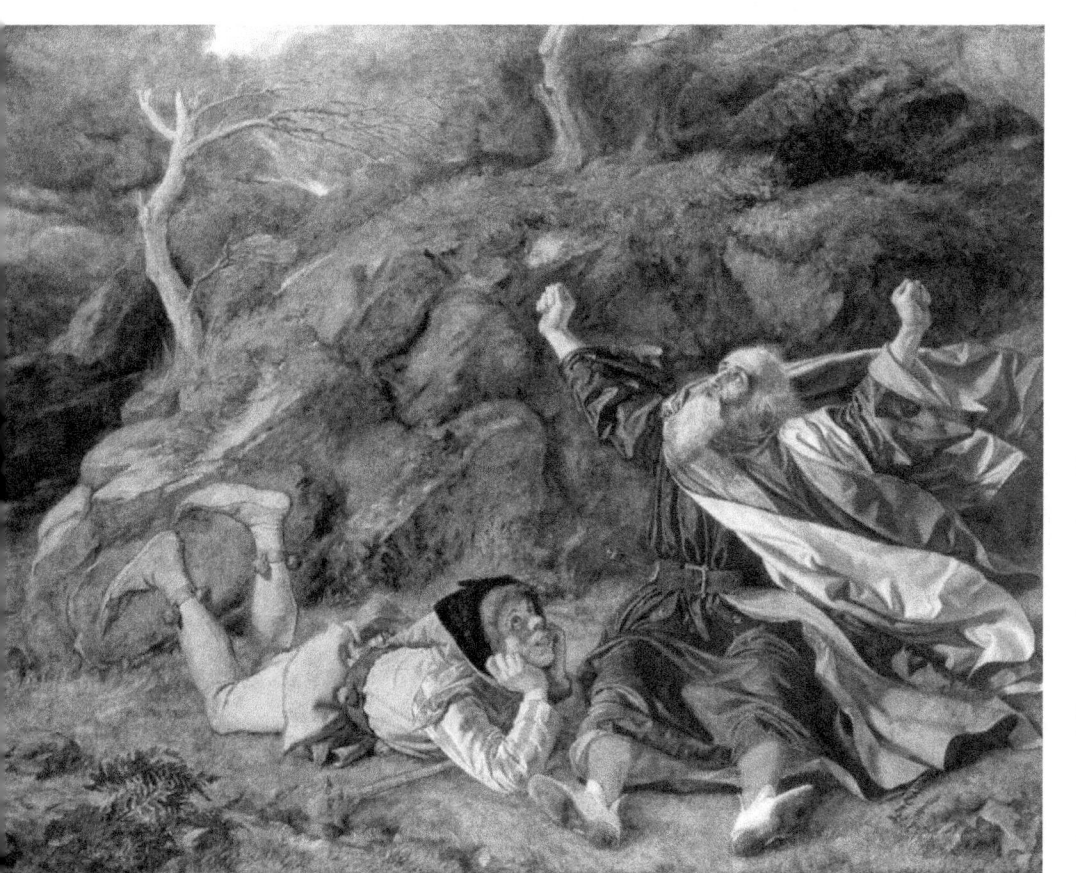

William Dyce, King Lear and the Fool In the Storm, 1851, Edinburgh

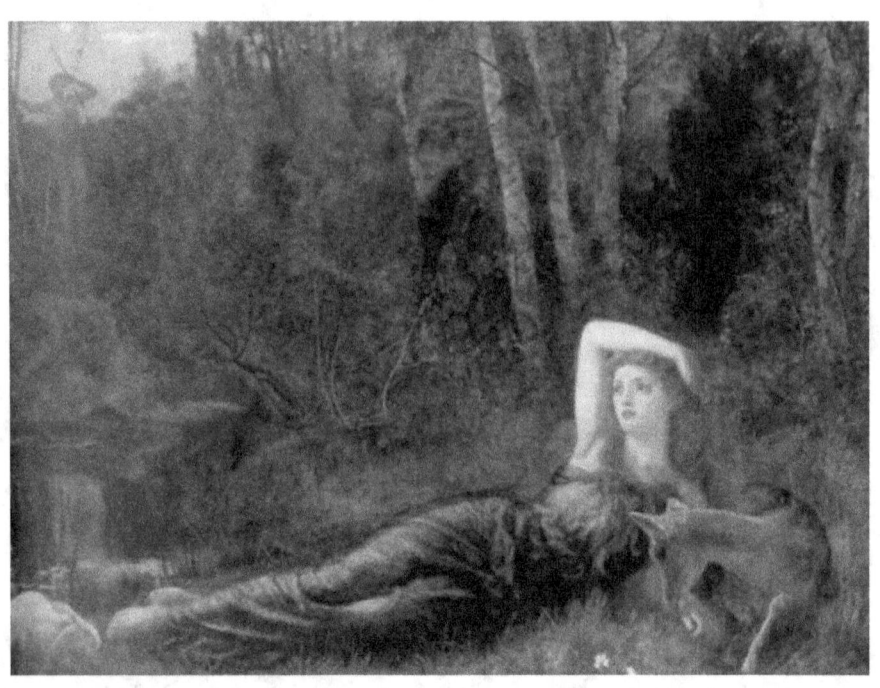

Arthur Hughes, Endymion

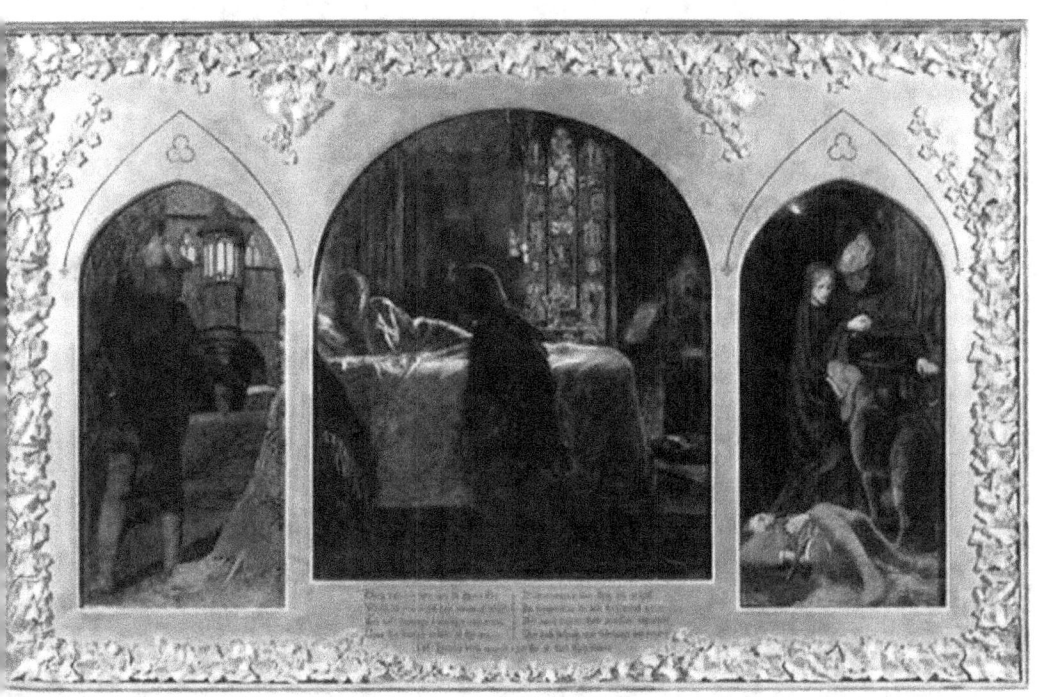

Arthur Hughes, The Eve of St Agnes

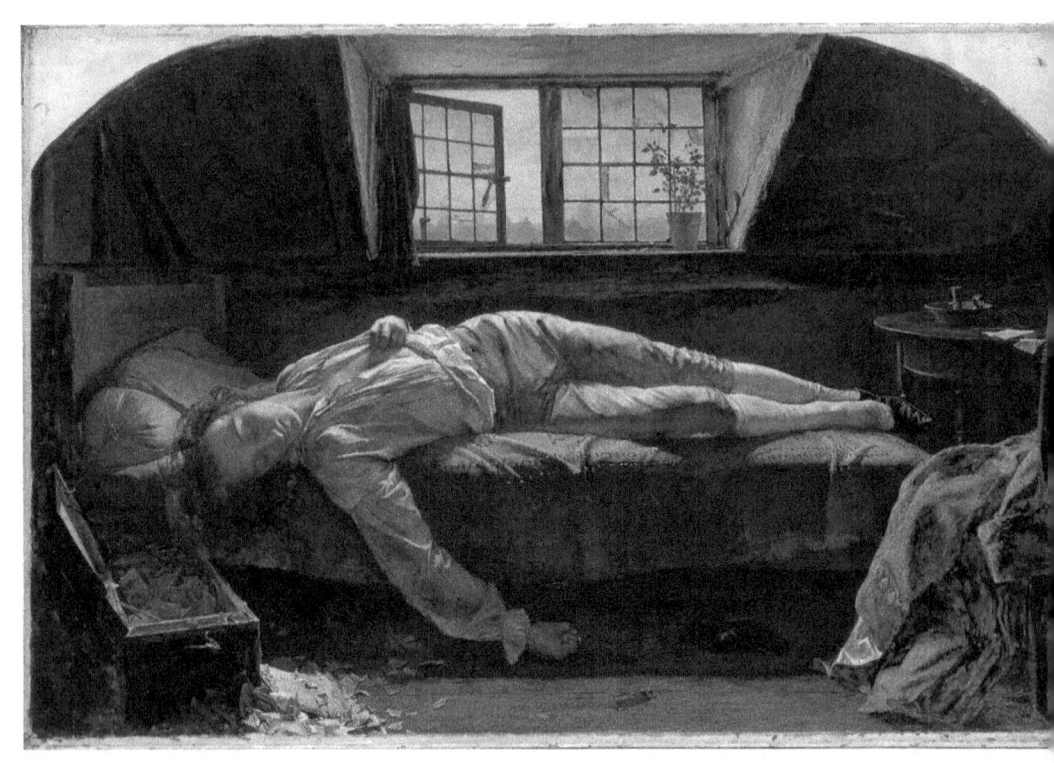

Henry Wallis, Chatterton, 1856, Tate Britain

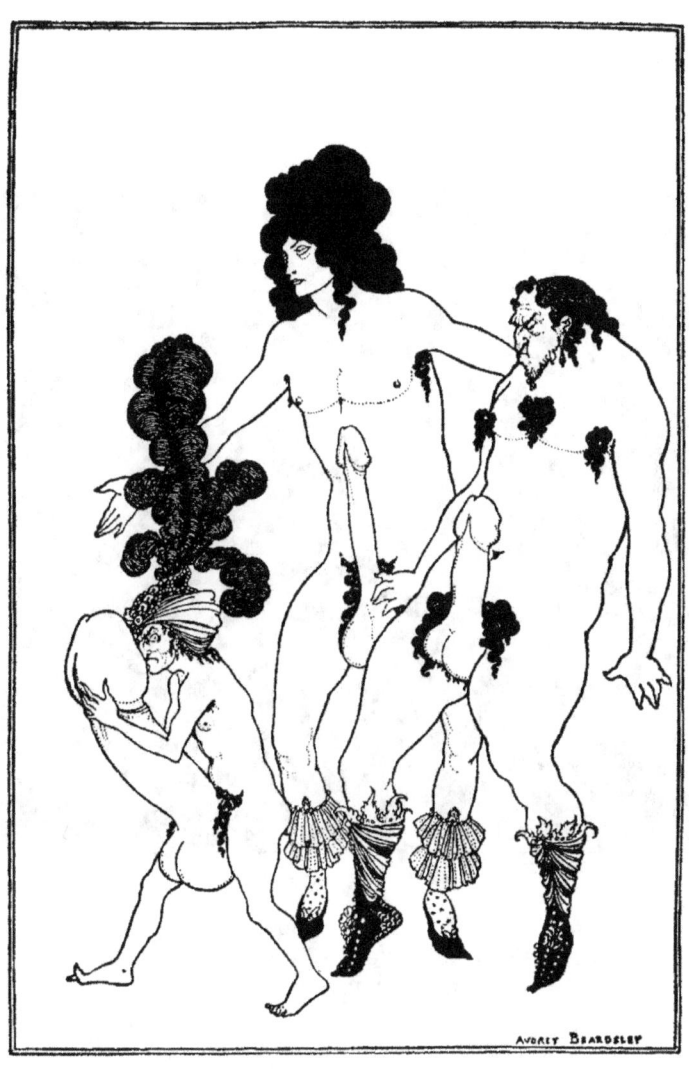

Aubrey Beardsley, Aristophanes, Lysistrata, 1896

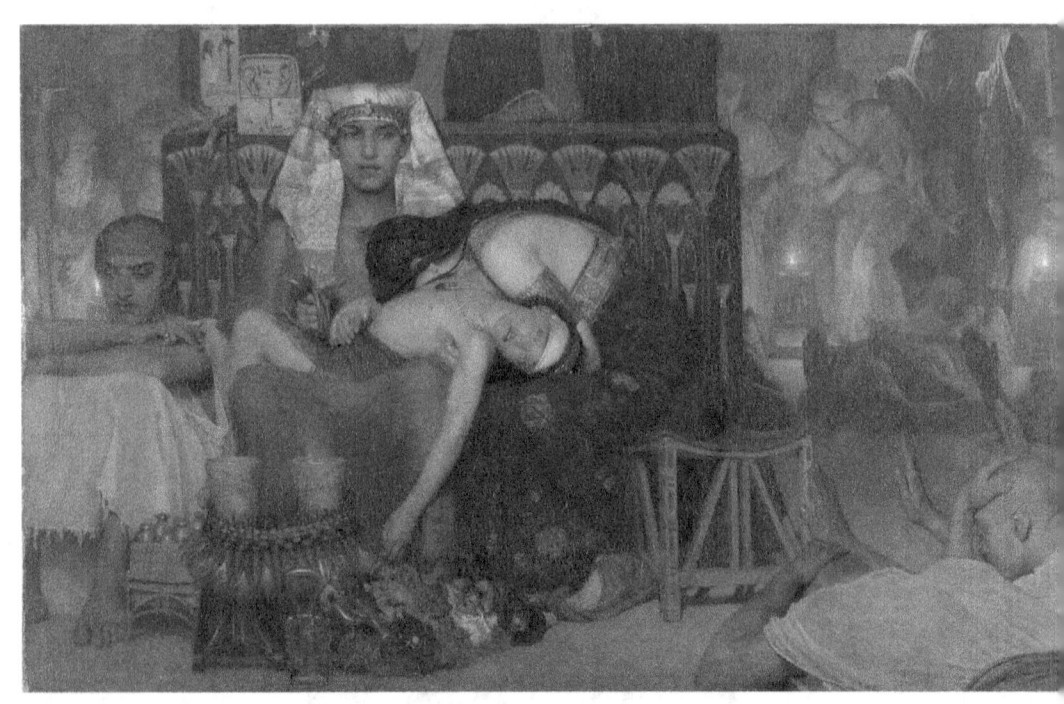

Lawrence Alma-Tadema,
The Death of the Pharaoh's Firstborn Son, 1872,
Rijksmuseum, Amsterdam

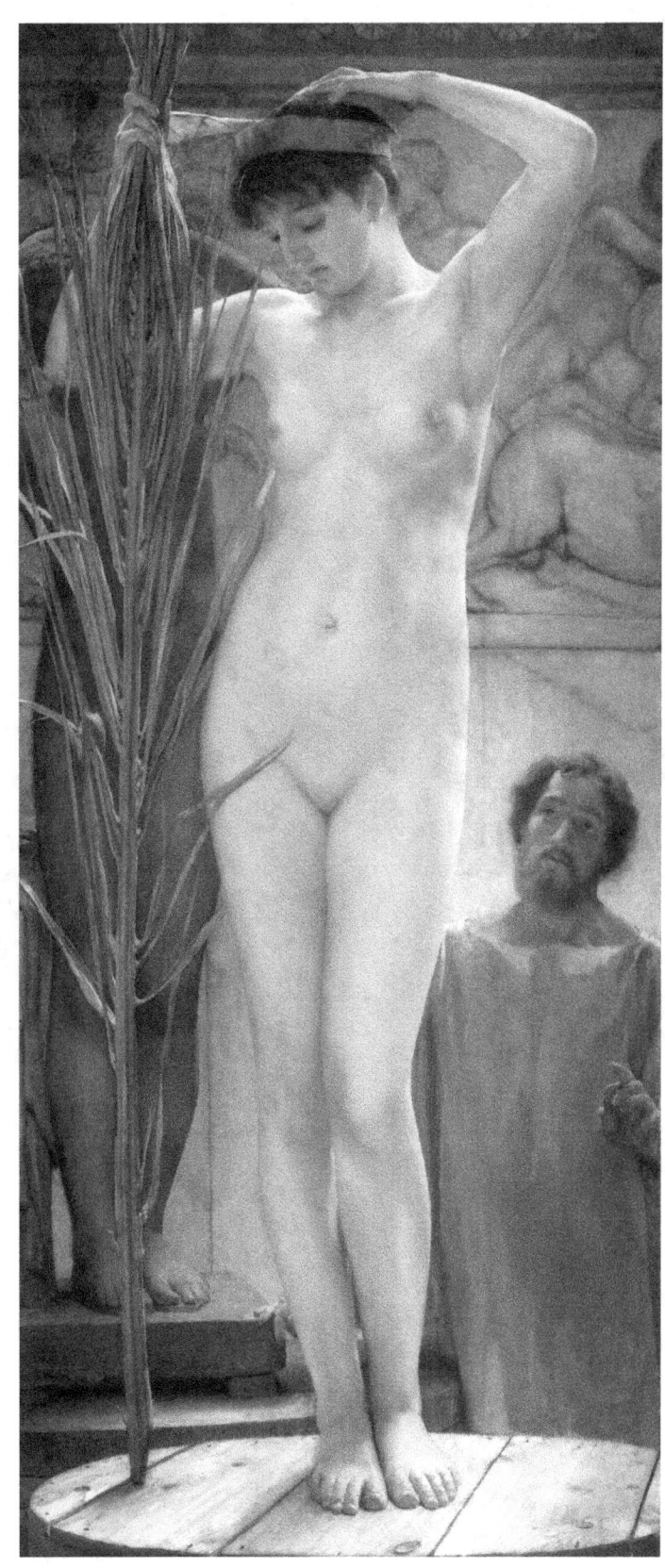

Lawrence
Alma-Tadema,
A Sculptor's Model,
1877, private
collection

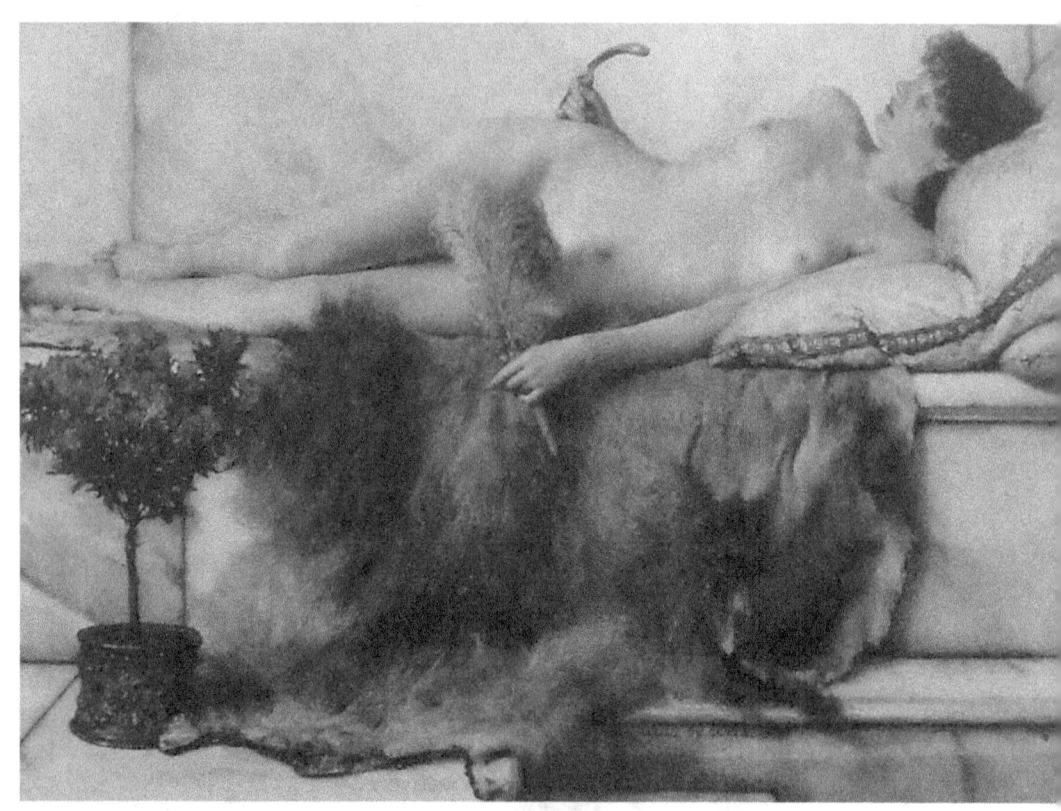

Lawrence Alma-Tadema, In the Tepidarium, 1881,
Lady Lever Art Gallery, Liverpool

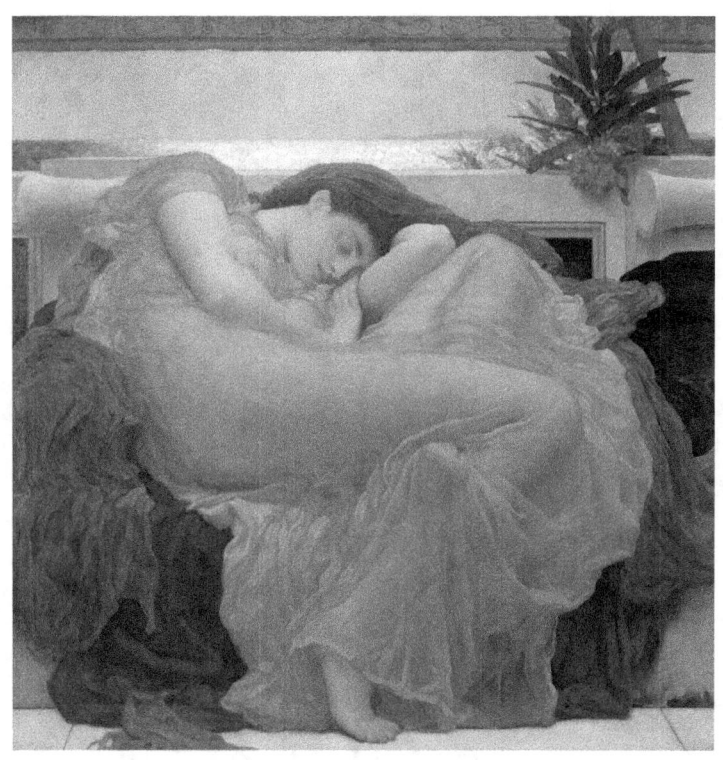

Lord Leighton, Flaming June, 1895, Puerto Rico

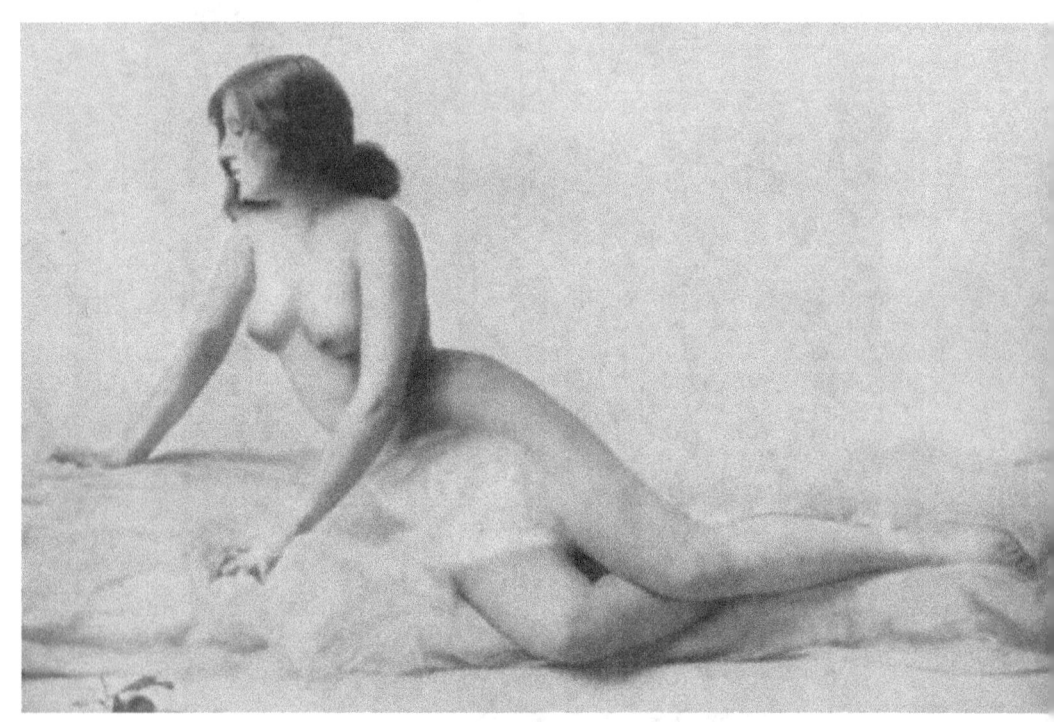

Frederick Armstrong, Greek Slave,
1909, drawn from Lord Leighton

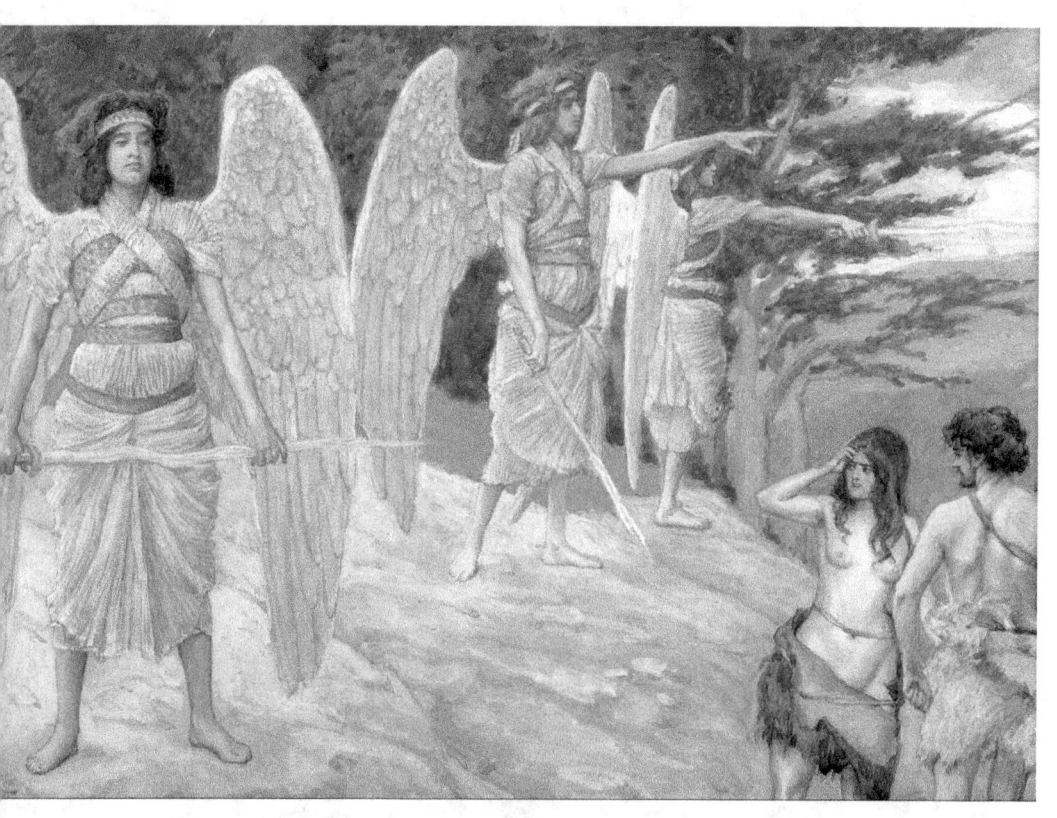

James Tissot, Adam and Eve Driven From Paradise, Jewish Museum, NYC

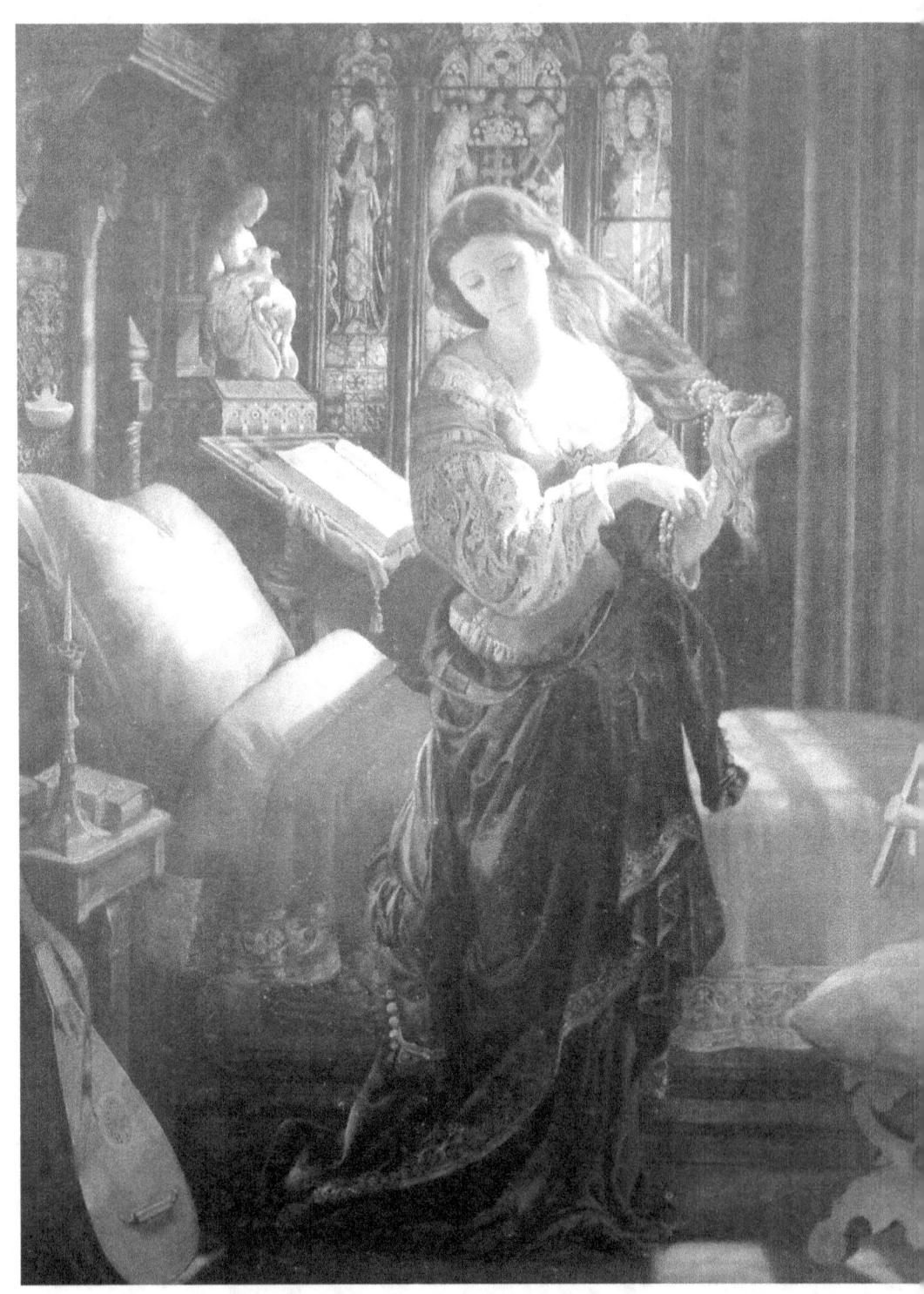

Daniel Maclise, Madeline After Prayer, 1868, Walker Art Gallery

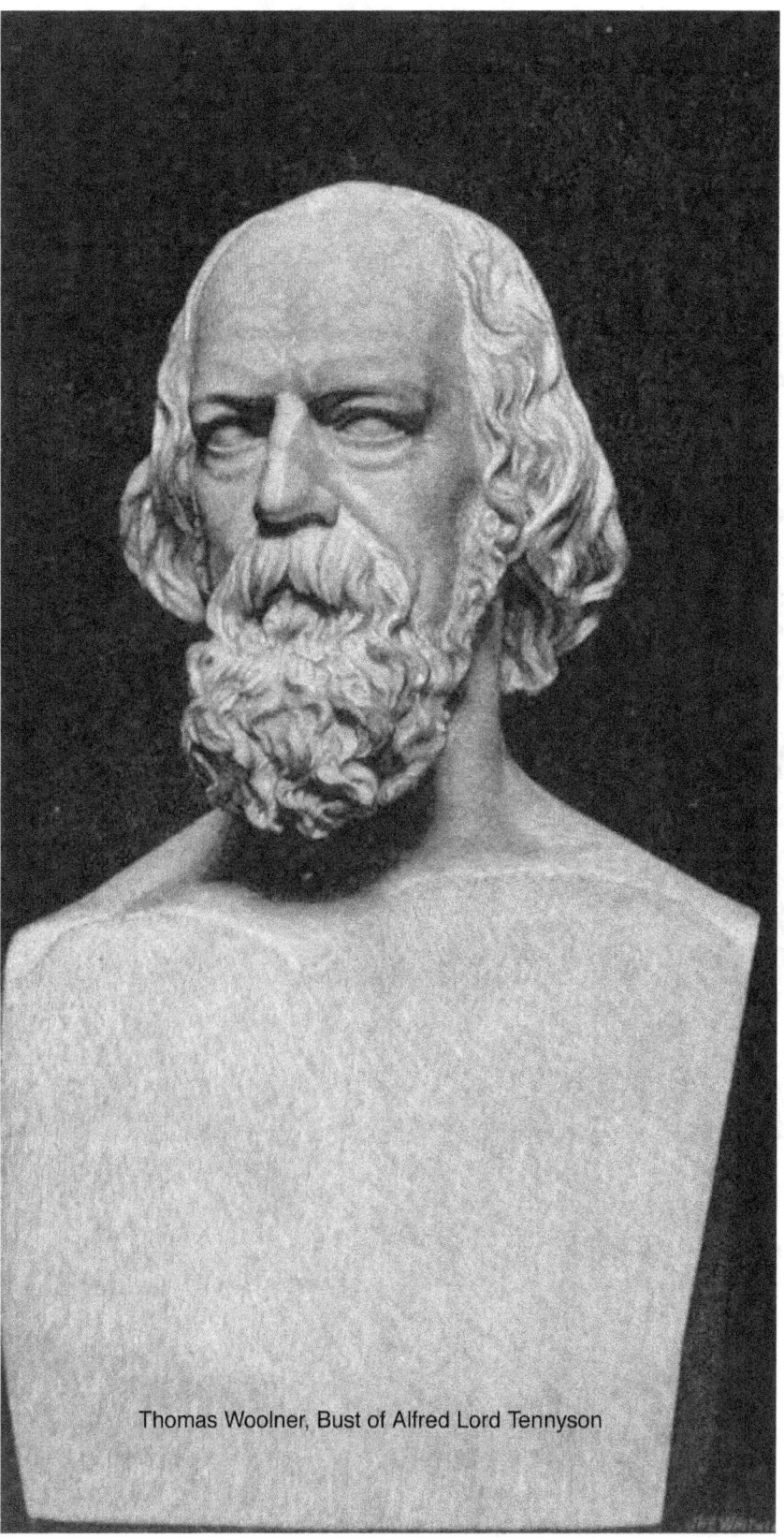

Thomas Woolner, Bust of Alfred Lord Tennyson

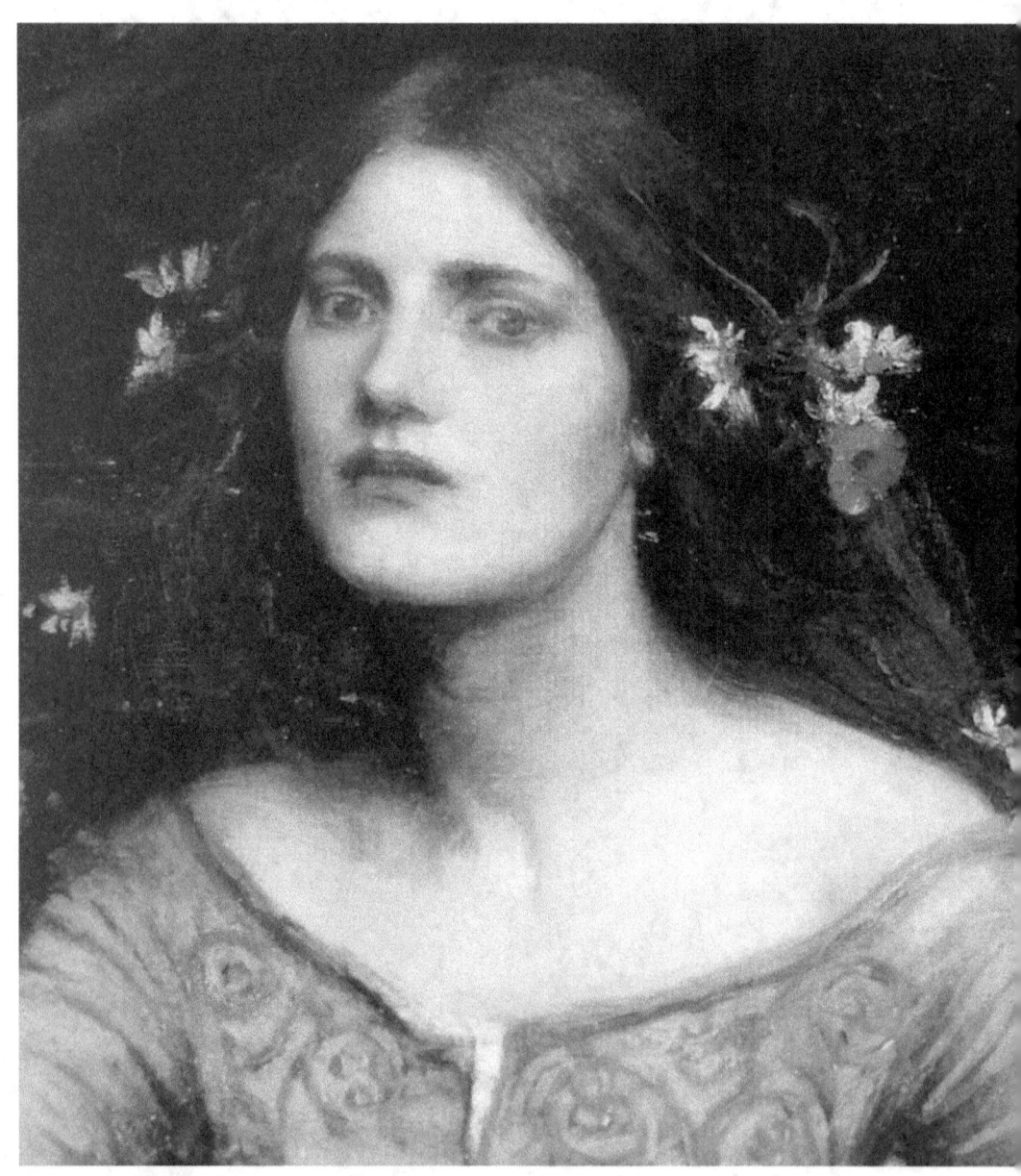

John William Waterhouse, Ophelia, 1910, detail

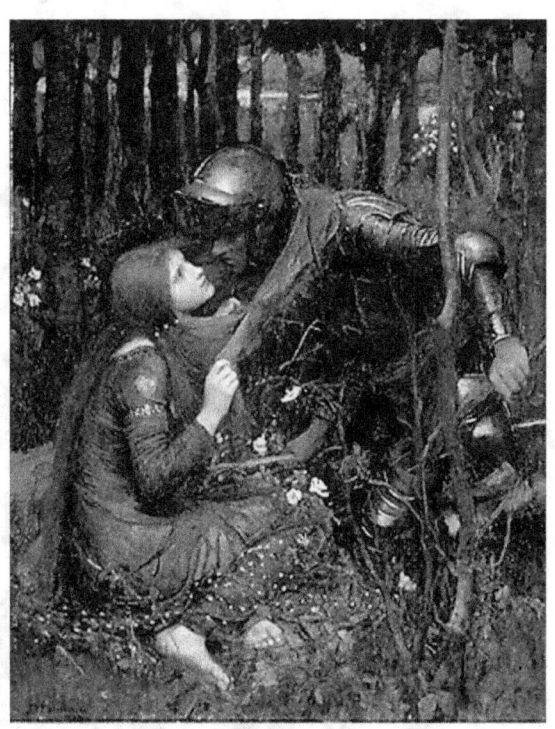

John Waterhouse, 'La Belle Dame Sans Merci'

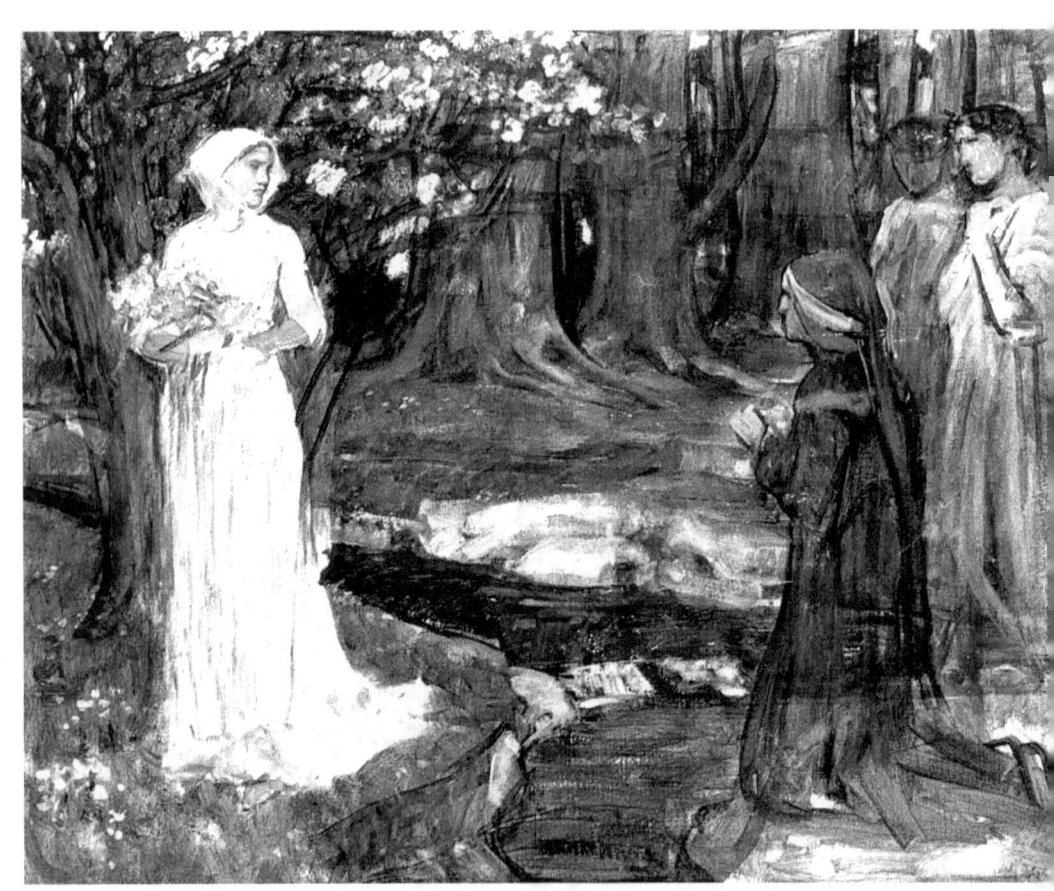

John William Waterhouse, Dante and Matilda, 1915,
Dahesh Museum of Art

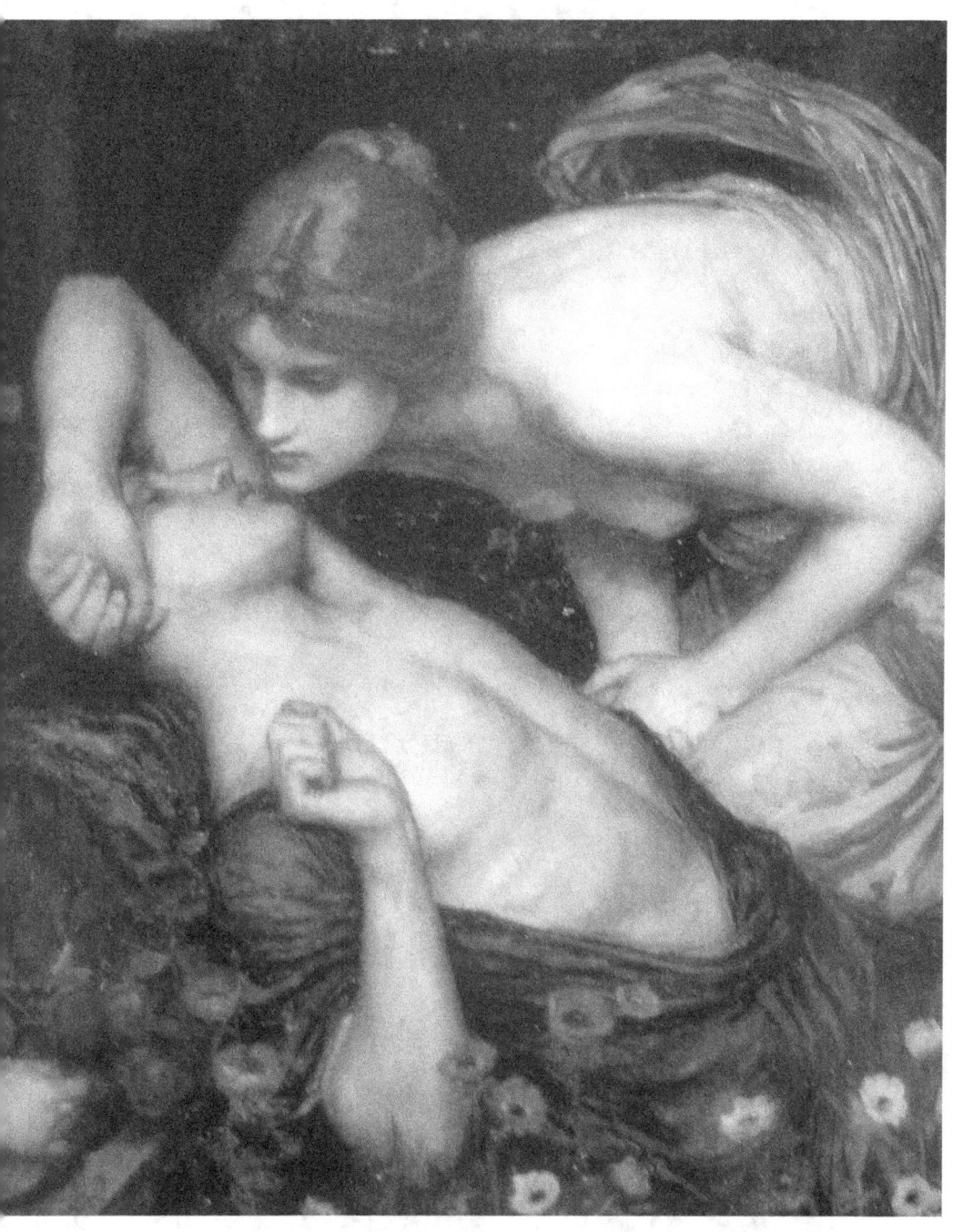

John William Waterhouse, The Awakening of Adonis, 1899, detail

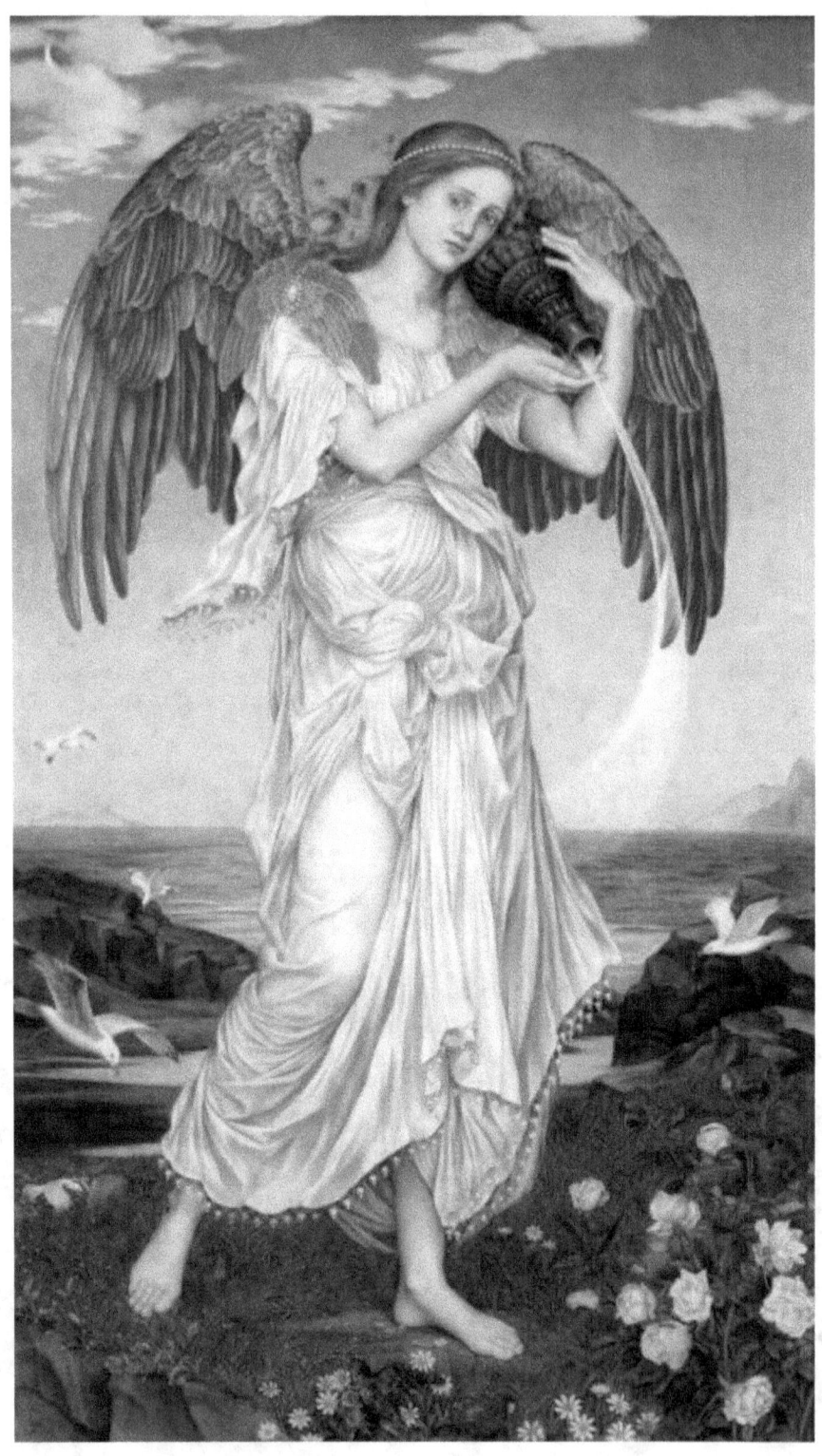

Evelyn de Morgan, Eos, 1895, Columbus, Ohio

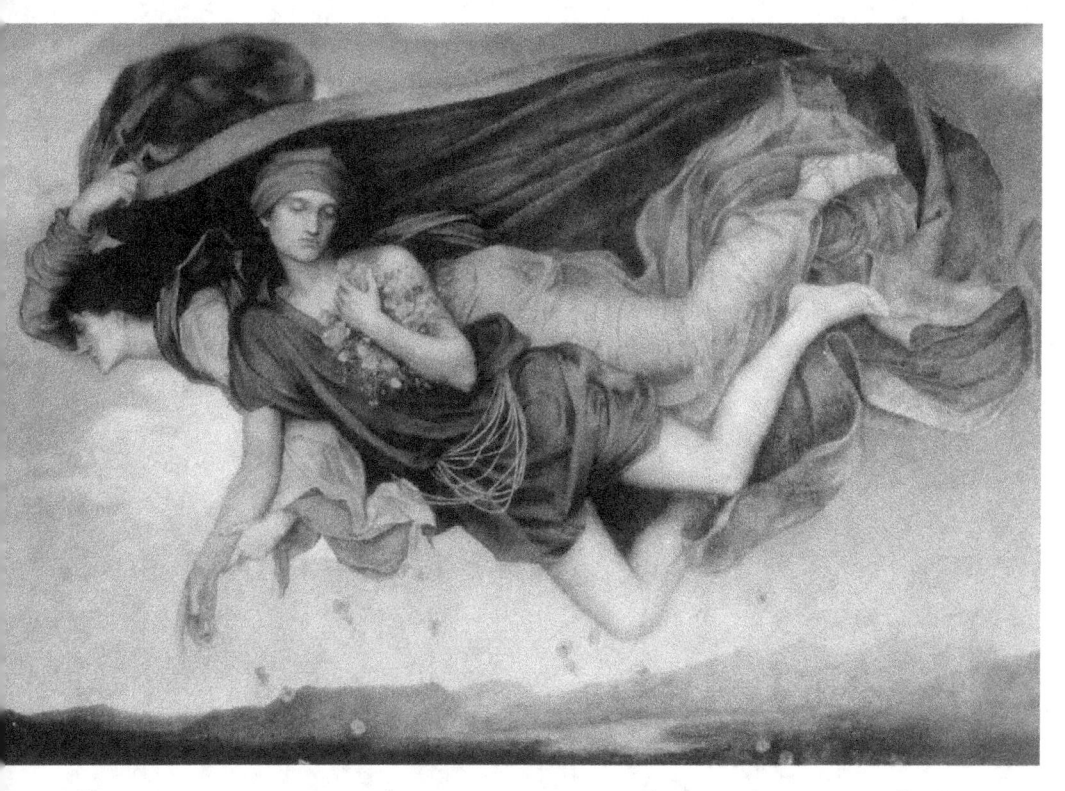

Evelyn de Morgan, Night and Sleep, 1878, Guildford

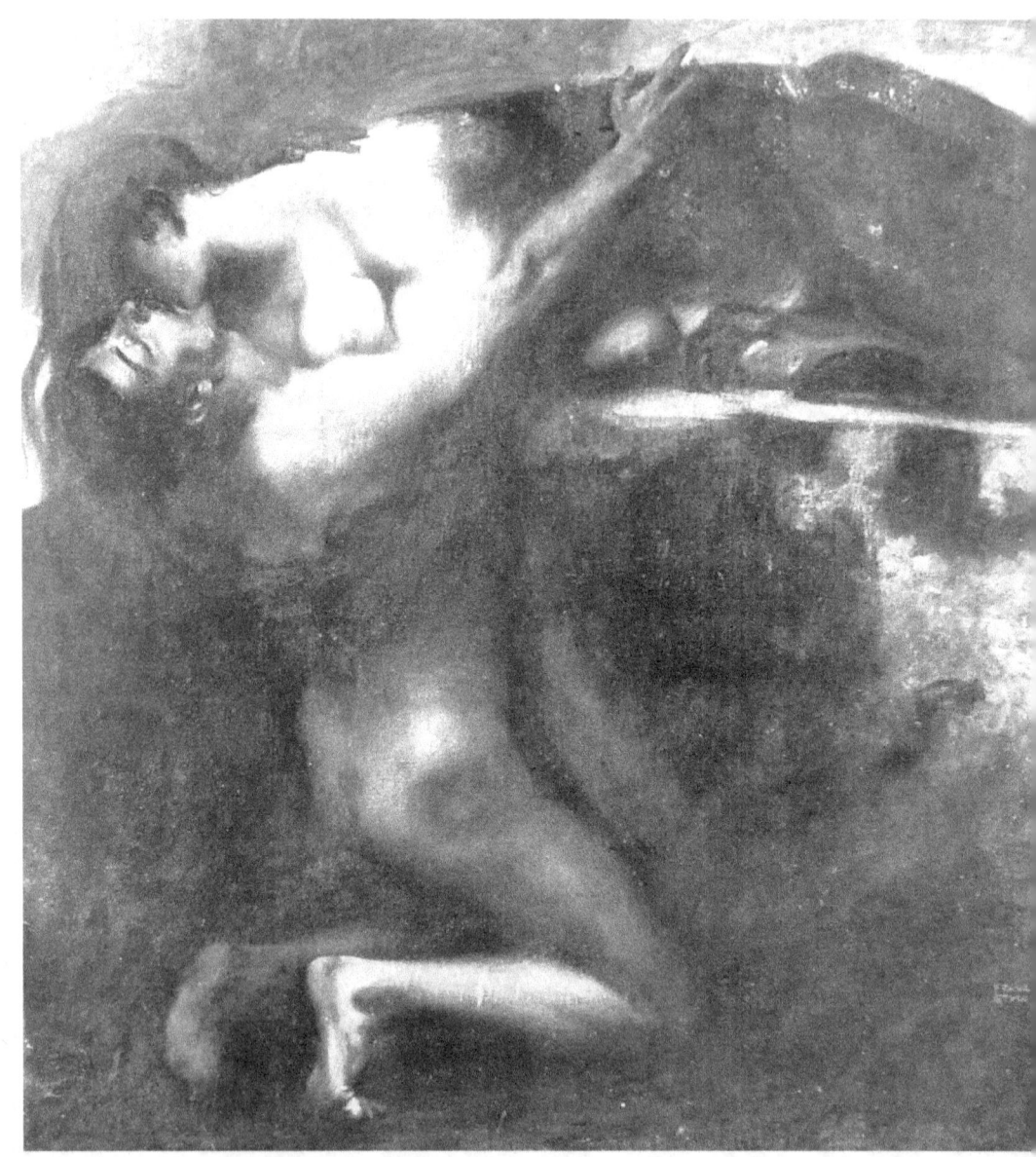

Franz von Stuck, Sphinx

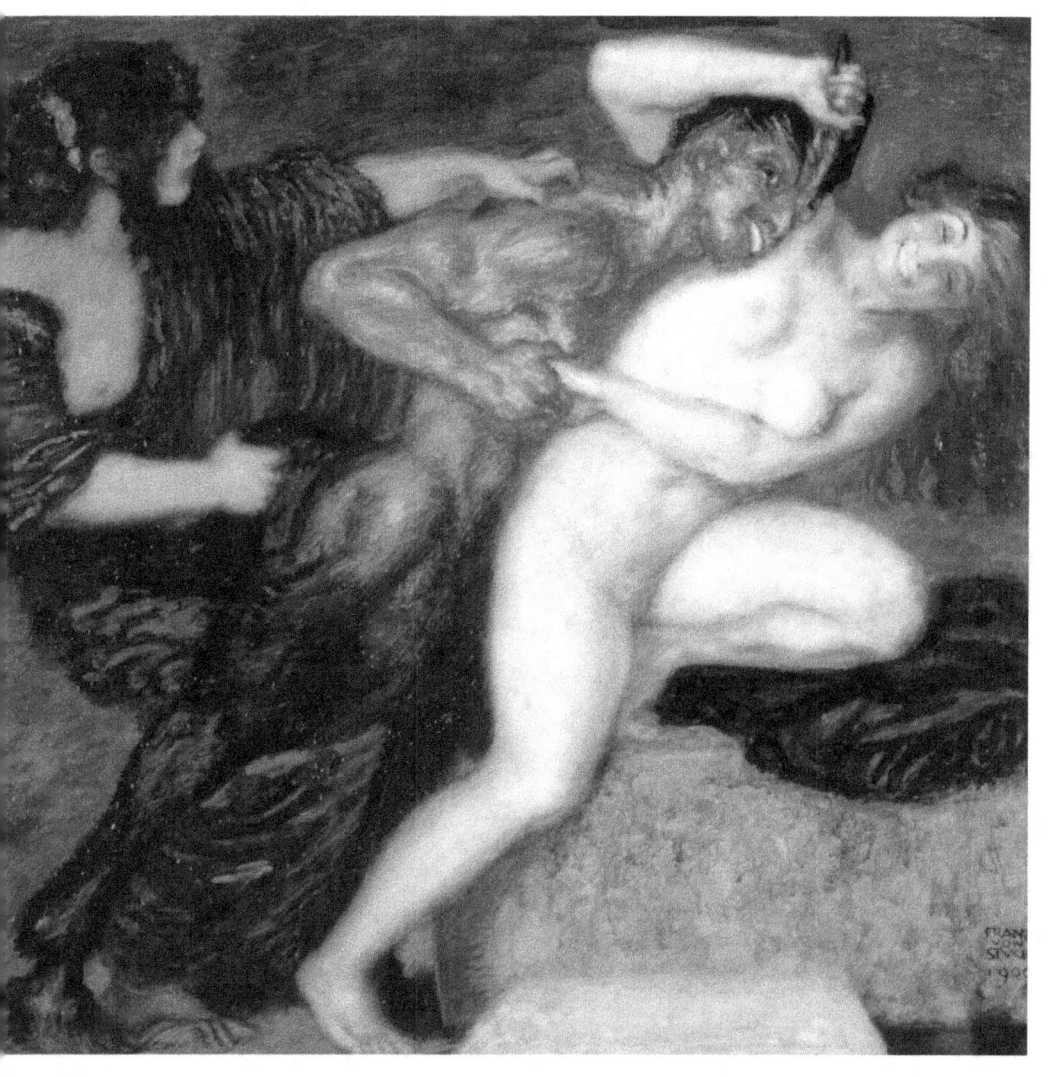

Franz von Stuck, Scherzo

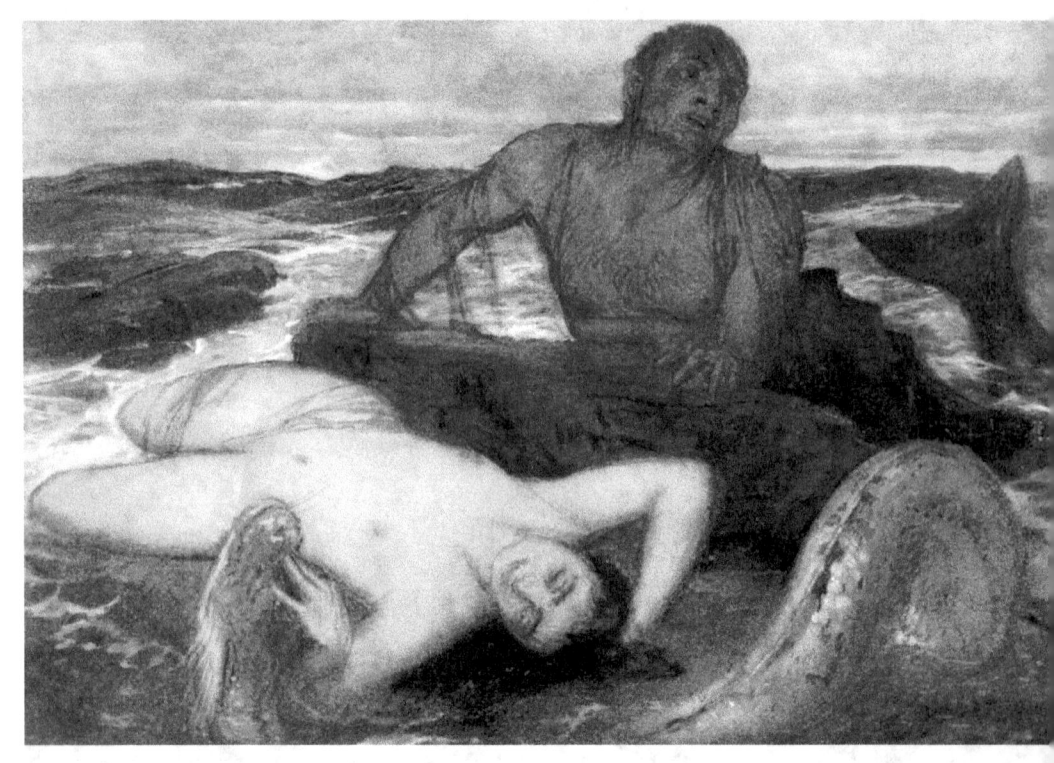

Arnold Böcklin, Triton and Nereid, 1877

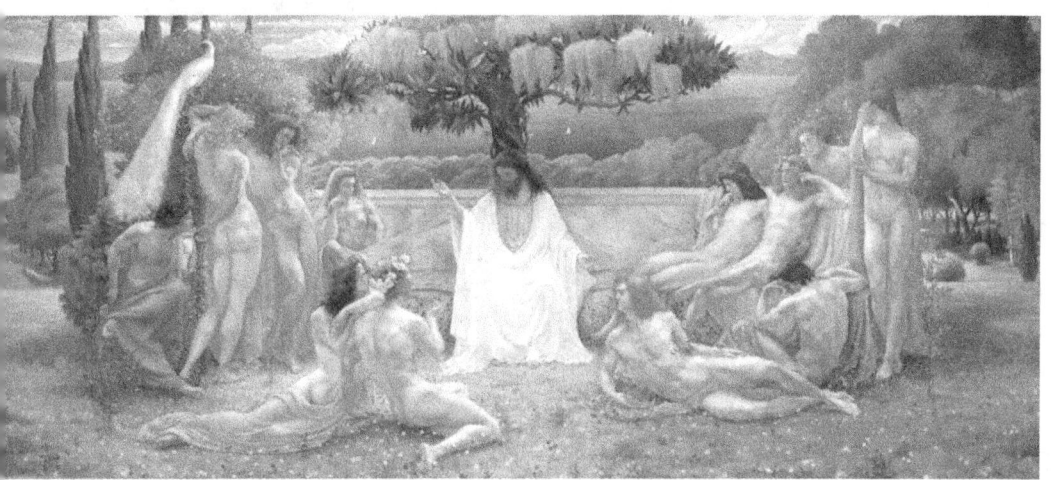

Jean Delville, The School of Plato, 1898

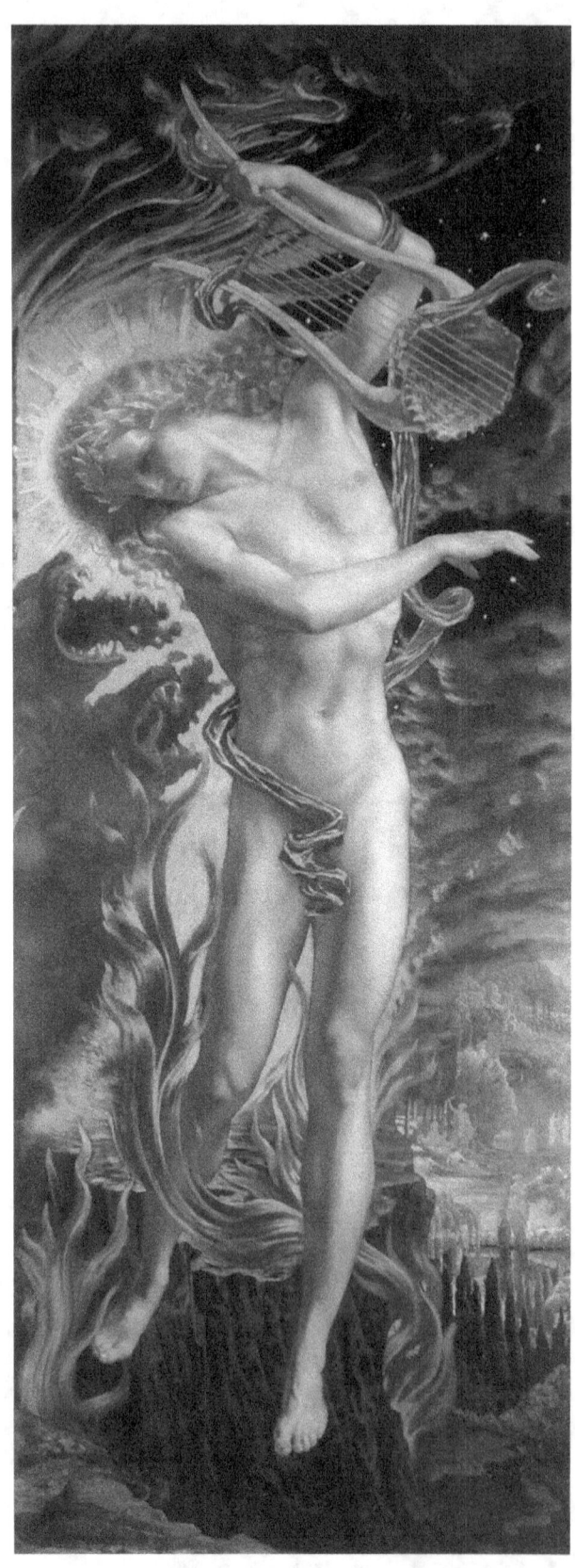

Jean Delville,
Orpheus,
late 19th century

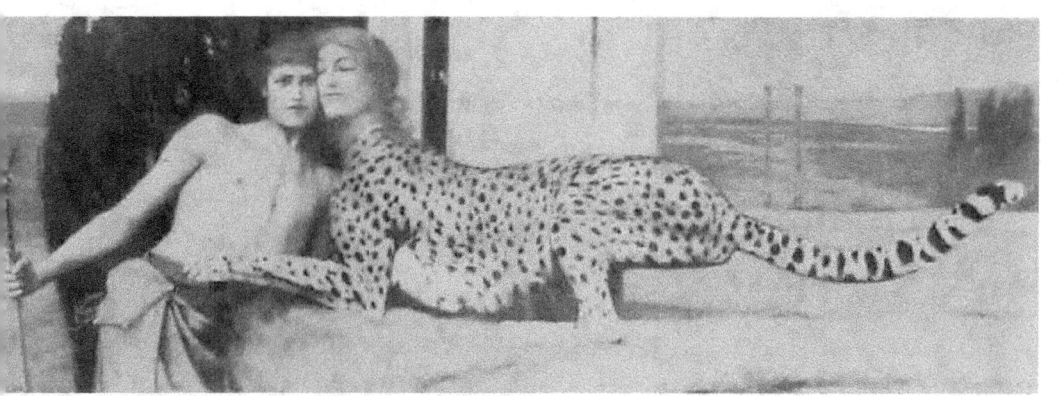

Fernand Knopff, The Caresses of the Sphinx, 1896, Brussels

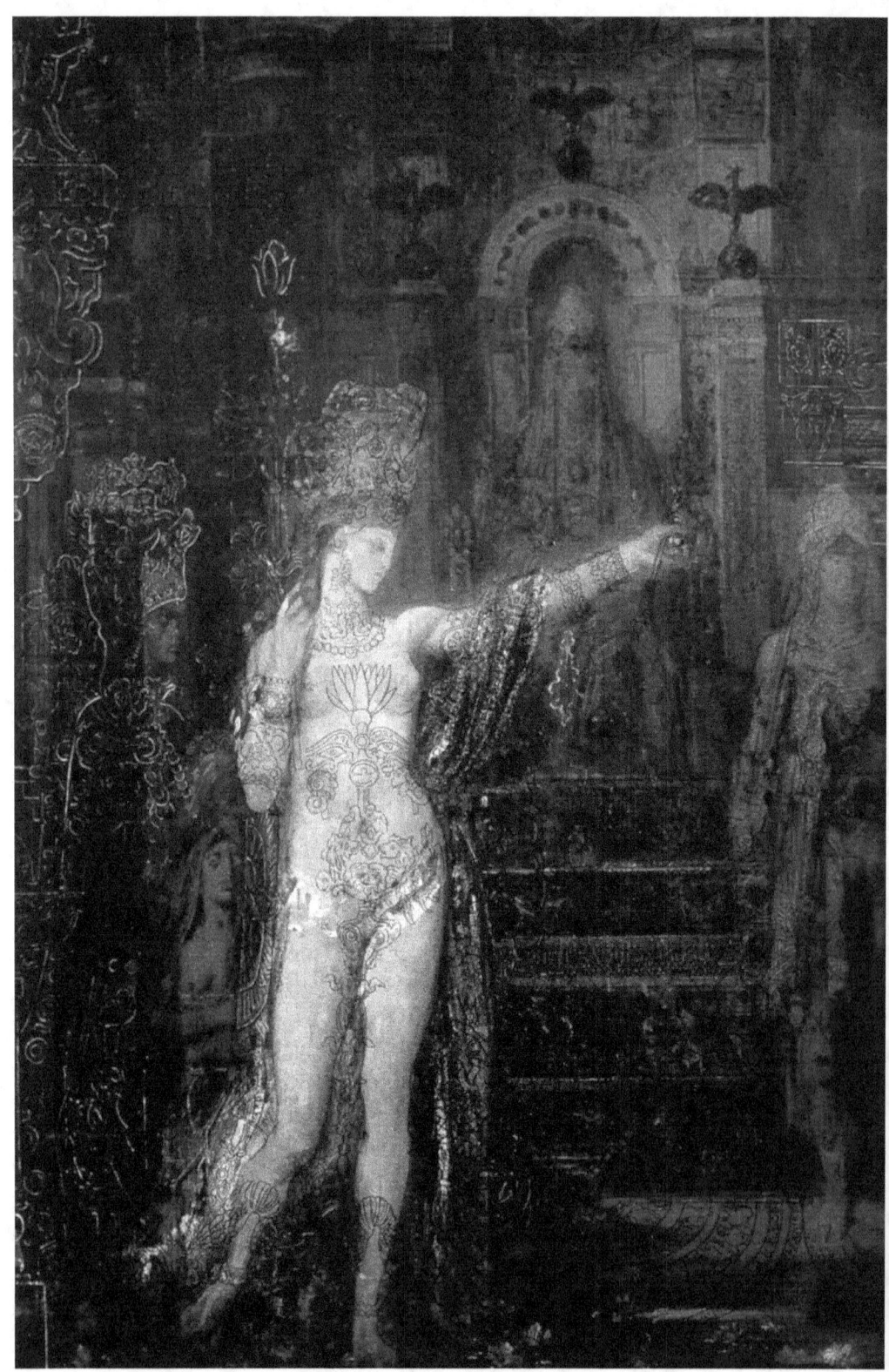

Gustave Moreau, Salomé, 1876

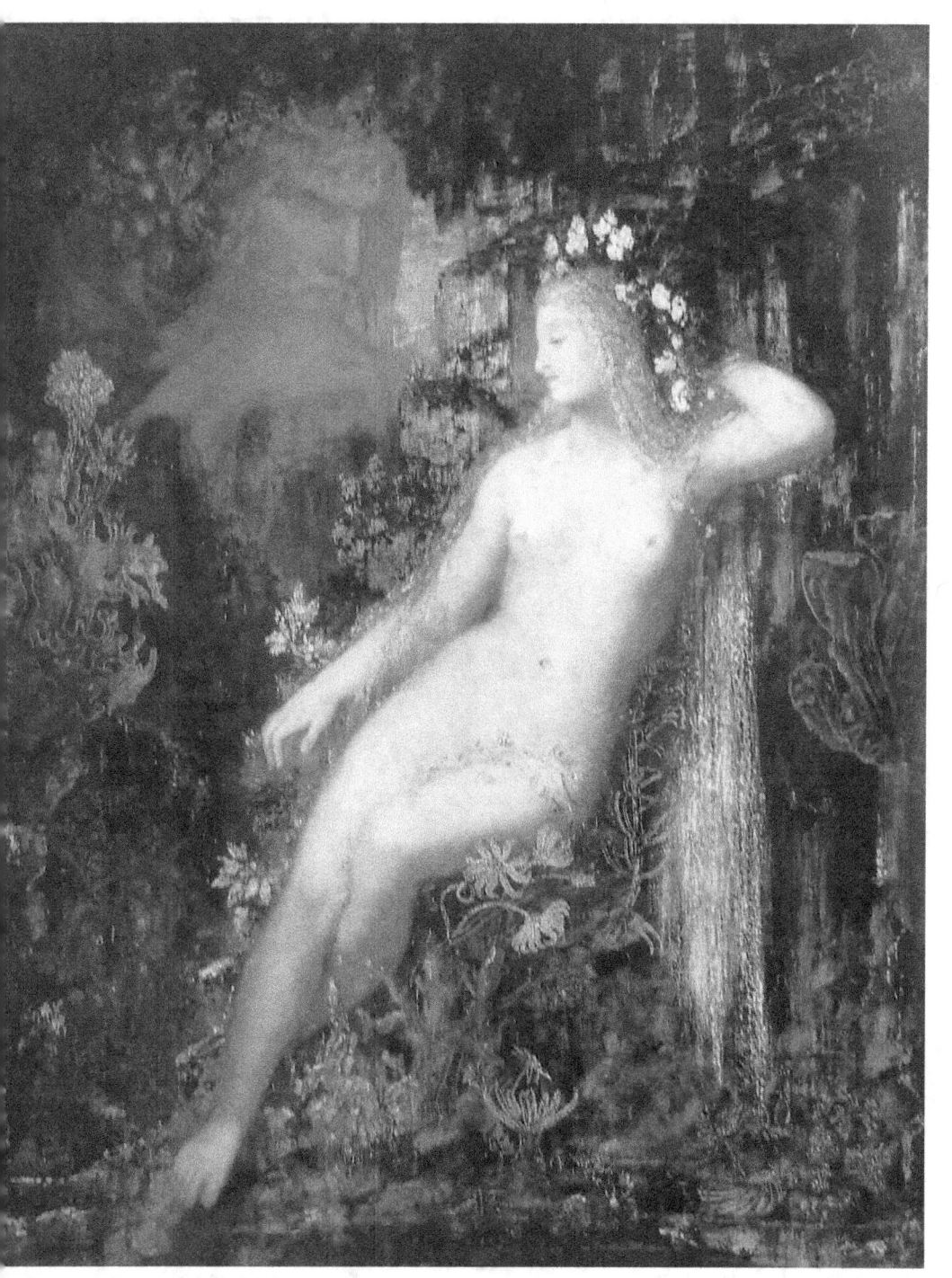

Gustave Moreau, Galatea, 1880

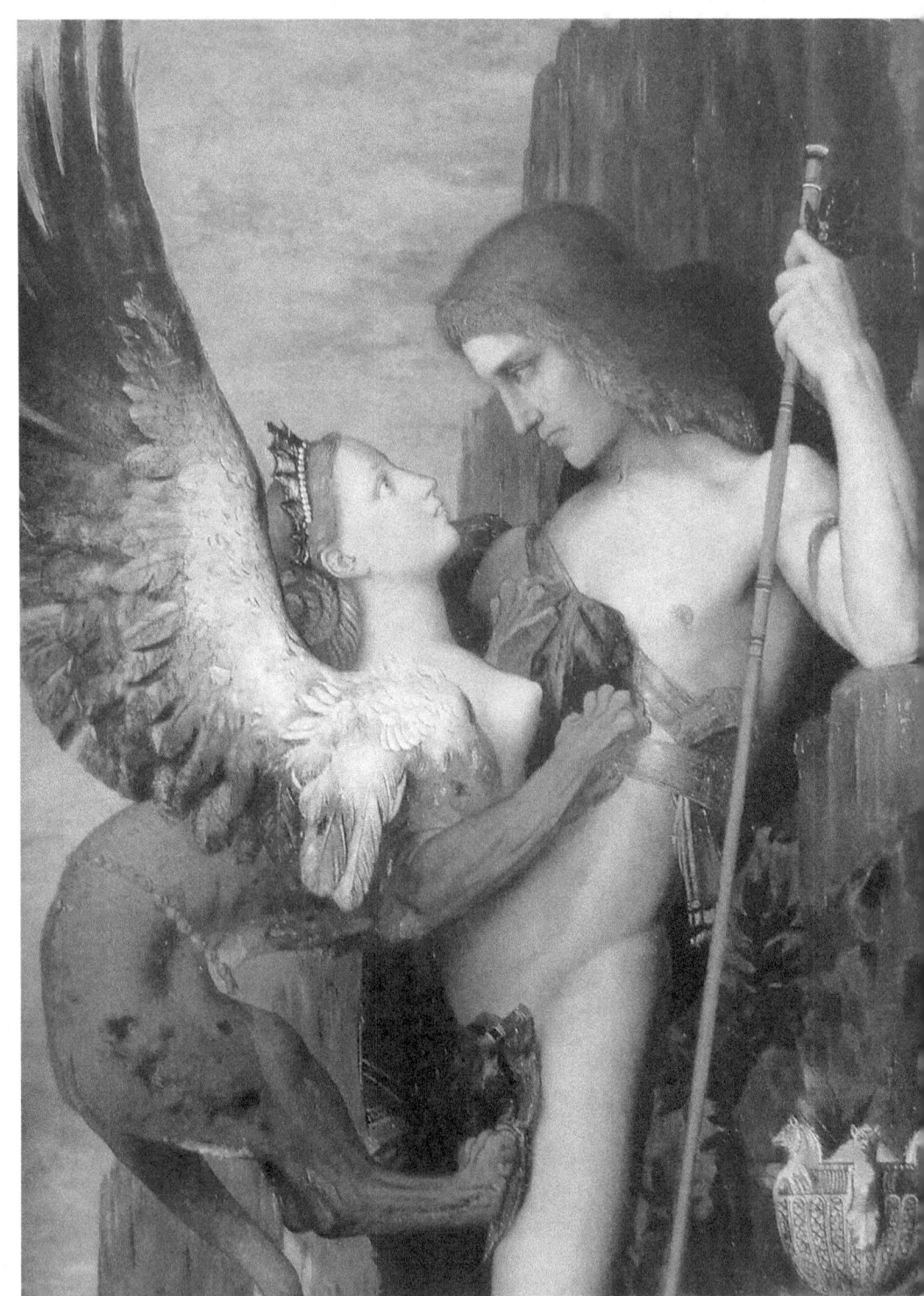

Gustave Moreau, The Sphinx

PRE-RAPHAELITISM

Delivered November 18, 1853.

The subject on which I would desire to engage your attention this evening, is the nature and probable result of a certain schism which took place a few years ago among our British artists.

This schism, or rather the heresy which led to it, as you are probably aware, was introduced by a small number of very young men; and consists mainly in the assertion that the principles on which art has been taught for these three hundred years back are essentially wrong, and that the principles which ought to guide us are those which prevailed before the time of Raphael; in adopting which, therefore, as their guides, these young men, as a sort of bond of unity among themselves, took the unfortunate and somewhat ludicrous name of "Pre-Raphaelite Brethren."

You must also be aware that this heresy has been opposed with all the influence and all the bitterness of art and criticism; but that in spite of these the heresy has gained ground, and the pictures painted on these new principles have obtained a most extensive popularity. These circumstances are sufficiently singular, but their importance is greater even than their singularity; and your time will certainly not be wasted in devoting an hour to an inquiry into the true nature of this movement.

I shall first, therefore, endeavor to state to you what the real difference is between the principles of art before and after Raphael's time, and then to ascertain, with you, how far these young men truly have understood the difference, and what may be hoped or feared from the effort they are making.

First, then, What is the real difference between the principles on which art has been pursued before and since Raphael? You must be aware, that the principal ground on which the Pre-Raphaelites have been attacked, is the charge that they wish to bring us back to a time of darkness and ignorance, when the principles of drawing, and of art in general, were comparatively unknown; and this attack, therefore, is entirely founded on the assumption that, although for some unaccountable reason we cannot at present produce artists altogether equal to Raphael, yet that we are on the whole in a state of greater illumination than, at all events, any artists who preceded Raphael; so that we consider ourselves entitled to look down upon them, and to say that, all things considered, they did some wonderful things for their time; but that, as for comparing the art of Giotto to that of Wilkie or Edwin Landseer, it would be perfectly ridiculous, – the one being a mere infant in his profession, and the others accomplished workmen.

Now, that this progress has in some things taken place is perfectly true; but it is true also that this progress is by no means the main thing to be noticed respecting ancient and modern art; that there are other circumstances, connected with the change from one to the other, immeasurably more important, and which, until very lately, have been altogether lost sight of.

The fact is, that modern art is not so much distinguished from old art by greater skill, as by a radical change in temper. The art of this day is not merely a more *knowing* art than that of the thirteenth century, – it is altogether another art. Between the two there is a great gulf, a distinction forever ineffaceable. The change from one to the other was not that of the child into the man, as we usually consider it; it was that of the chrysalis into the butterfly. There was an entire change in the habits, food, method of existence, and heart of the whole creature. That we know more than thirteenth century people is perfectly true; but that is not the essential difference between us and them. We are different kind of creatures from them, – as different as moths are different from caterpillars; and different in a certain broad and vast sense, which I shall try this evening to explain and prove to you; – different not merely in this or that result of minor circumstances, – not as you are different from people who never saw a locomotive engine, or a Highlander of this century from a Highlander of 1745; – different in a far broader and mightier sense than that; in a sense so great and clear, that we are enabled to separate all the Christian nations and tongues of the early time from those of the latter time, and speak of them in one group as the kingdoms of the Middle Ages. There is an infinite significance in that term, which I want you to dwell upon and work out; it is a term which we use in a dim consciousness of the truth, but without fully penetrating into that of which we are conscious. I want to deepen and make clear to you this consciousness that the world has had essentially a Trinity of ages – the Classical Age, the Middle Age, the Modern Age; each of these embracing races and individuals of apparently enormous separation in kind, but united in the spirit of their age, – the Classical Age having its Egyptians and Ninevites, Greeks and Romans, – the Middle Age having its Goths and Franks, Lombards and Italians, – the Modern Age having its French and English, Spaniards and Germans; but all these distinctions being in each case subordinate to the mightier and broader distinction, between *Classicalism*, *Mediævalism*, and *Modernism*.

Now our object to-night is indeed only to inquire into a matter of art; but we cannot do so properly until we consider this art in its relation to the inner spirit of the age in which it exists; and by doing so we shall not only arrive at the most just conclusions respecting our present subject, but we shall obtain the means of arriving at just conclusions respecting many other things.

Now the division of time which the Pre-Raphaelites have adopted, in choosing Raphael as the man whose works mark the separation between Mediævalism and Modernism, is perfectly accurate. It has been accepted as such by all their opponents.

You have, then, the three periods: Classicalism, extending to the fall of the Roman empire; Mediævalism, extending from that fall to the close of the fifteenth century; and Modernism thenceforward to our days.

And in examining into the spirit of these three epochs, observe, I don't mean to compare their bad men, – I don't mean to take Tiberius as a type of Classicalism, nor Ezzelin as a type of Mediævalism, nor Robespierre as a type of Modernism. Bad men are like each other in all epochs; and in the Roman, the Paduan, or the Parisian, sensuality and cruelty admit of little distinction in the manners of their manifestation. But among men comparatively virtuous, it is important to study the phases of character; and it is into these only that it is necessary for us to inquire. Consider therefore, first, the essential difference in character between three of the most devoted military heroes whom the three great epochs of the world have produced, – all three devoted to the service of their country, – all of them dying therein. I mean, Leonidas in the Classical period, St. Louis in the Mediæval period, and Lord Nelson in the Modern period.

Leonidas had the most rigid sense of duty, and died with the most perfect faith in the gods of his country, fulfilling the accepted prophecy of his death. St. Louis had the most rigid sense of duty, and the most perfect faith in Christ. Nelson had the most rigid sense of duty, and –

You must supply my pause with your charity.

Now you do not suppose that the main difference between Leonidas and Nelson lay in the modern inventions at the command of the one, as compared with the imperfect military instruments possessed by the other. They were not essentially different, in that the one fought with lances and the other with guns. But they were essentially different in the whole tone of their religious belief.

By this instance you may be partially prepared for the bold statement I am going to make to you, as to the change which constitutes Modernism. I said just now that it was like that of the worm to the butterfly. But the changes which God causes in His lower creatures are almost always from worse to better, while the changes which God allows man to make in himself are very often quite the other way; like Adam's new arrangement of his nature. And in saying that this last change was like that of a chrysalis, I meant only in the completeness of it, not in the tendency of it. Instead of from the worm to the butterfly, it is very possible it may have been from the butterfly to the worm.

Have patience with me for a moment after I tell you what I

believe it to have been, and give me a little time to justify my words.

I say that Classicalism began, wherever civilization began, with Pagan Faith. Mediævalism began, and continued, wherever civilization began and continued to *confess* Christ. And, lastly, Modernism began and continues, wherever civilization began and continues to *deny* Christ.

You are startled, but give me a moment to explain. What, you would say to me, do you mean to tell us that *we* deny Christ? we who are essentially modern in every one of our principles and feelings, and yet all of us professing believers in Christ, and we trust most of us true ones? I answer, So far as we are believers indeed, we are one with the faithful of all times, – one with the classical believer of Athens and Ephesus, and one with the mediæval believer of the banks of the Rhone and the valleys of the Monte Viso. But so far as, in various strange ways, some in great and some in small things, we deny this belief, in so far we are essentially infected with this spirit, which I call Modernism.

For observe, the change of which I speak has nothing whatever to do with the Reformation, or with any of its effects. It is a far broader thing than the Reformation. It is a change which has taken place, not only in reformed England, and reformed Scotland; but in unreformed France, in unreformed Italy, in unreformed Austria. I class honest Protestants and honest Roman Catholics for the present together, under the general term Christians: if you object to their being so classed together, I pray your pardon, but allow me to do so at present, for the sake of perspicuity, if for nothing else; and so classing them, I say that a change took place, about the time of Raphael, in the spirit of Roman Catholics and Protestants both; and that change consisted in the *denial* of their religious belief, at least in the external and trivial affairs of life, and often in far more serious things.

For instance, hear this direction to an upholsterer of the early thirteenth century. Under the commands of the Sheriff of Wiltshire, he is thus ordered to make some alterations in a room for Henry the Third. He is to "wainscot the King's lower chamber, and to paint that wainscot of a green color, and to put a border to it, and to cause the heads of kings and queens to be painted on the borders; and to paint on the walls of the King's upper chamber the story of St. Margaret, Virgin, and the four Evangelists, and to paint the wainscot of the same chamber of a green color, spotted with gold."[1]

Again, the Sheriff of Wiltshire is ordered to "put two small glass windows in the chamber of Edward the King's son; and put a glass window in the chamber of our Queen at Clarendon; and in the same window cause to be painted a Mary with her Child, and at the feet of the said Mary, a queen with clasped hands."

Again, the Sheriff of Southampton is ordered to "paint the tablet beside the King's bed, with the figures of the guards of the bed of Solomon, and to glaze with white glass the windows in the King's great Hall at Northampton, and cause the history of Lazarus and Dives to be painted in the same."

And so on; I need not multiply instances. You see that in all these cases, the furniture of the King's house is made to confess his Christianity. It may be imperfect and impure Christianity, but such as it might be, it was all that men had then to live and die by; and you see there was not a pane of glass in their windows, nor a pallet by their bedside that did not confess and proclaim it. Now, when you go home to your own rooms, supposing them to be richly decorated at all, examine what that decoration consists of. You will find Cupids, Graces, Floras, Dianas, Jupiters, Junos. But you will not find, except in the form of an engraving, bought principally for its artistic beauty, either Christ, or the Virgin, or Lazarus and Dives. And if a thousand years hence, any curious investigator were to dig up the ruins of Edinburgh, and not know your history, he would think you had all been born heathens. Now that, so far as it goes, is denying Christ; it is pure Modernism.

"No," you will answer me, "you misunderstand and calumniate us. We do not, indeed, choose to have Dives and

Lazarus on our windows; but that is not because we are moderns, but because we are Protestants, and do not like religious imagery." Pardon me: that is not the reason. Go into any fashionable lady's boudoir in Paris, and see if you will find Dives and Lazarus there. You will find, indeed, either that she has her private chapel, or that she has a crucifix in her dressing-room; but for the general decoration of the house, it is all composed of Apollos and Muses, just as it is here.

Again. What do you suppose was the substance of good education, the education of a knight, in the Middle Ages? What was taught to a boy as soon as he was able to learn anything? First, to keep under his body, and bring it into subjection and perfect strength; then to take Christ for his captain, to live as always in His presence, and finally, to do his *devoir* - mark the word - to all men. Now consider, first, the difference in their influence over the armies of France, between the ancient word "devoir," and modern word "gloire." And, again, ask yourselves what you expect your own children to be taught at your great schools and universities. Is it Christian history, or the histories of Pan and Silenus? Your present education, to all intents and purposes, denies Christ, and that is intensely and peculiarly Modernism.

Or, again, what do you suppose was the proclaimed and understood principle of all Christian *governments* in the Middle Ages? I do not say it was a principle acted up to, or that the cunning and violence of wicked men had not too often their full sway then as now; but on what principles were that cunning and violence, so far as was possible, restrained? By the *confessed* fear of God, and *confessed* authority of His law. You will find that all treaties, laws, transactions whatsoever, in the Middle Ages, are based on a confession of Christianity as the leading rule of life; that a text of Scripture is held, in all public assemblies, strong enough to be set against an appearance of expediency; and although, in the end, the expediency might triumph, yet it was never without a distinct allowance of Christian principle, as an efficient element in the consultation. Whatever error might be committed, at least Christ was openly confessed. Now what is the custom of your British Parliament in these days? You know that nothing would excite greater manifestations of contempt and disgust than the slightest attempt to introduce the authority of Scripture in a political consultation. That is denying Christ. It is intensely and peculiarly Modernism.

It would be easy to go on showing you this same thing in many more instances; but my business to-night is to show you its full effect in one thing only, namely, in art, and I must come straightway to that, as I have little enough time. This, then, is the great and broad fact which distinguishes modern art from old art; that all ancient art was *religious*, and all modern art is *profane*. Once more, your patience for an instant. I say, all ancient art was religious; that is to say, religion was its first object; private luxury or pleasure its second. I say all modern art is profane; that is, private luxury or pleasure is its first object; religion its second. Now you all know, that anything which makes religion its second object, makes religion *no* object. God will put up with a great many things in the human heart, but there is one thing He will *not* put up with in it – a second place. He who offers God a second place, offers Him no place. And there is another mighty truth which you all know, that he who makes religion his first object, makes it his whole object; he has no other work in the world than God's work. Therefore I do not say that ancient art was *more* religious than modern art. There is no question of degree in this matter. Ancient art was religious art; modern art is profane art; and between the two the distinction is as firm as between light and darkness.

Now, do not let what I say be encumbered in your minds with the objection, that you think art ought not to be brought into the service of religion. That is not the question at present – do not agitate it. The simple fact is, that old art *was* brought into that service, and received therein a peculiar form; that modern art *is not* brought into that service, and has received in consequence another form; that this is the great distinction between mediæval and modern art; and from that are clearly deducible all other essential differences between them. That is the point I wish to show you, and of that there can be no dispute. Whether or not Christianity be the purer for lacking the service of art, is disputable – and I do not mean now to begin the dispute; but that art is the *impurer* for not being in the service of Christianity, is indisputable, and that is the main point I have now to do with.

Perhaps there are some of you here who would not allow that the religion of the thirteenth century was Christianity. Be it so; still is the statement true, which is all that is necessary for me now to prove, that art was great because it was devoted to such religion as then existed. Grant that Roman Catholicism was not Christianity – grant it, if you will, to be the same thing as old heathenism – and still I say to you, whatever it was, men lived and died by it, the ruling thought of all their thoughts; and just as classical art was greatest in building to its gods, so mediæval art was great in building to its gods, and modern art is not great, because it builds to *no* God. You have, for instance, in your Edinburgh Library, a Bible of the thirteenth century, the Latin Bible, commonly known as the Vulgate. It contains the Old and New Testaments, complete, besides the books of Maccabees, the Wisdom of Solomon, the books of Judith, Baruch, and Tobit. The whole is written in the most beautiful black-letter hand, and each book begins with an illuminated letter, containing three or four figures, illustrative of the book which it begins. Now, whether this were done in the service of true Christianity or not, the simple fact is, that here is a man's life-time taken up in writing and ornamenting a Bible, as the sole end of his art; and that doing this, either in a book or on a wall, was the common artist's life at the time; that the constant Bible reading and Bible thinking which this work involved, made a man serious and thoughtful, and a good workman, because he was always expressing those feelings which, whether right or wrong, were the groundwork of his whole being. Now, about the year 1500, this entire system was changed. Instead of the life of Christ, men had, for the most part, to paint the lives of Bacchus and Venus; and if you walk through any public gallery of pictures by the "great masters," as they are called, you will indeed find here and there what is called a Holy Family, painted for the sake of drawing pretty children, or a pretty woman; but for the most part you will find nothing but Floras, Pomonas, Satyrs, Graces, Bacchanals, and Banditti. Now, you will not declare – you cannot believe – that Angelico painting the life of Christ, Benozzo painting the life of Abraham, Ghirlandajo painting the life of the Virgin, Giotto painting the life of St. Francis, were worse employed, or likely to produce a less healthy art, than Titian painting the loves of Venus and Adonis, than Correggio painting the naked Antiope, than Salvator painting the slaughters of the thirty years' war? If you will not let me call the one kind of labor Christian, and the other unchristian, at least you will let me call the one moral, and the other immoral, and that is all I ask you to admit.

Now observe, hitherto I have been telling you what you may feel inclined to doubt or dispute; and I must leave you to consider the subject at your leisure. But henceforward I tell you plain facts, which admit neither of doubt nor dispute by any one who will take the pains to acquaint himself with their subject-matter.

When the entire purpose of art was moral teaching, it naturally took truth for its first object, and beauty, and the pleasure resulting from beauty, only for its second. But when it lost all purpose of moral teaching, it as naturally took beauty for its first object, and truth for its second.

That is to say, in all they did, the old artists endeavored, in one way or another, to express the real facts of the subject or event, this being their chief business: and the question they first asked themselves was always, how would this thing, or that, actually have occurred? what would this person, or that, have done under the circumstances? and then, having formed their conception, they work it out with only a secondary regard to grace or beauty, while a modern painter invariably thinks of the grace and beauty of his work first, and unites afterwards as much truth as he can with its conventional graces. I will give you a single strong instance to make my meaning plainer. In Orcagna's great fresco of the Triumph of Death, one of the incidents is that three kings,[2] when out hunting, are met by a spirit, which, desiring them to follow it, leads them to a churchyard, and points out to them, in open coffins, three bodies of kings such as themselves, in the last stages of corruption. Now a modern artist, representing this, would have endeavored dimly and faintly to suggest the appearance of the dead bodies, and would have made, or attempted to make, the countenances of the three kings variously and solemnly expressive of thought. This would be in his, or our, view, a poetical and tasteful treatment of the subject. But Orcagna disdains both poetry and taste; he wants the *facts* only; he wishes to give the spectator the same lesson that the kings had; and therefore, instead of concealing the dead bodies, he paints them with the most fearful detail. And then, he does not consider what the three kings might most gracefully do. He considers only what they actually in all probability *would have done*. He makes them looking at the coffins with a startled stare, and one holding his nose. This is an extreme instance; but you are not to suppose it is because Orcagna had naturally a coarse or prosaic mind. Where he felt that thoughtfulness and beauty could properly be introduced, as in his circles of saints and prophets, no painter of the Middle Ages is so grand. I can give you no better proof of this, than the one fact that Michael Angelo borrowed from him openly – borrowed from him in the principal work which he ever executed, the Last Judgment, and borrowed from him the principal figure in that work. But it is just because Orcagna was so firmly and unscrupulously true, that he had the power of being so great when he chose. His arrow went straight to the mark. It was not that he did not love beauty, but he loved truth first.

So it was with all the men of that time. No painters ever had more power of conceiving graceful form, or more profound devotion to the beautiful; but all these gifts and affections are kept sternly subordinate to their moral purpose; and, so far as their powers and knowledge went, they either painted from nature things as they were, or from imagination things as they must have been.

I do not mean that they reached any imitative resemblance to nature. They had neither skill to do it, nor care to do it. Their art was conventional and imperfect, but they considered it only as a language wherein to convey the knowledge of certain facts; it was perfect enough for that; and though always reaching on to greater attainments, they never suffered their imperfections to disturb and check them in their immediate purposes. And this mode of treating all subjects was persisted in by the greatest men until the close of the fifteenth century.

Now so justly have the Pre-Raphaelites chosen their time and name, that the great change which clouds the career of mediæval art was affected, not only in Raphael's time, but by Raphael's own practice, and by his practice in *the very center of his available life*.

You remember, doubtless, what high ground we have for placing the beginning of human intellectual strength at about the age of twelve years.[3] Assume, therefore, this period for the beginning of Raphael's strength. He died at thirty-seven. And in his twenty-fifth year, one half-year only past the precise center of his available life, he was sent for to Rome, to decorate the Vatican for Pope Julius II., and having until that time worked exclusively in the ancient and stern mediæval manner, he, in the first chamber which he decorated in that palace, wrote upon its walls the *Mene, Tekel, Upharsin* of the Arts of Christianity.

And he wrote it thus: On one wall of that chamber he placed a picture of the World or Kingdom of *Theology*, presided over by *Christ*. And on the side wall of that same chamber he placed the World or Kingdom of *Poetry*, presided over by *Apollo*. And from that spot, and from that hour, the intellect and the art of Italy date their degradation.

Observe, however, the significance of this fact is not in the mere use of the figure of the heathen god to indicate the domain of poetry. Such a symbolical use had been made of the figures of heathen deities in the best times of Christian art. But it is in the fact, that being called to Rome especially to adorn the palace of the so-called head of the Church, and called as the chief representative of the Christian artists of his time, Raphael had neither religion nor originality enough to trace the spirit of poetry and the spirit of philosophy to the inspiration of the true God, as well as that of theology; but that, on the contrary, *he elevated the creations of fancy on the one wall, to the same rank as the objects of faith upon the other*; that in deliberate, balanced opposition to the Rock of the Mount Zion, he reared the rock of Parnassus, and the rock of the Acropolis; that, among the masters of poetry we find him enthroning Petrarch and Pindar, but not Isaiah nor David, and for lords over the domain of philosophy we find the masters of the school of Athens, but neither of those greater masters by the last of whom that school was rebuked, – those who received their wisdom from heaven itself, in the vision of Gibeon,[4] and the lightning of Damascus.

The doom of the arts of Europe went forth from that chamber, and it was brought about in great part by the very excellencies of the man who had thus marked the commencement of decline. The perfection of execution and the beauty of feature which were attained in his works, and in those of his great contemporaries, rendered finish of execution and beauty of form the chief objects of all artists; and thenceforward execution was looked for rather than thought, and beauty rather than veracity.

And as I told you, these are the two secondary causes of the decline of art; the first being the loss of moral purpose. Pray note them clearly. In mediæval art, thought is the first thing, execution the second; in modern art execution is the first thing, and thought the second. And again, in mediæval art, truth is first, beauty second; in modern art, beauty is first, truth second. The mediæval principles led *up* to Raphael, and the modern principles lead *down* from him.

Now, first, let me give you a familiar illustration of the difference with respect to execution. Suppose you have to teach two children drawing, one thoroughly clever and active-minded, the other dull and slow; and you put before them Jullien's chalk studies of heads – *études à deux crayons* – and desire them to be copied. The dull child will slowly do your bidding, blacken his paper and rub it white again, and patiently and painfully, in the course of three or four years, attain to the performance of a chalk head, not much worse than his original, but still of less value than the paper it is drawn upon. But the clever child will not, or will only by force, consent to this discipline. He finds other means of expressing himself with his pencil somehow or another; and presently you find his paper covered with sketches of his grandfather and grandmother, and uncles, and cousins – sketches of the room, and the house, and the cat, and the dog, and the country outside, and everything in the world he can set his eyes on; and he gets on, and even his child's work has a value in it – a truth which makes it worth keeping; no one knows how precious, perhaps, that portrait of his grandfather may be, if any one has but the sense to keep it till the time when the old man can be seen no more up the lawn, nor by the wood. That child is working in the Middle-Age spirit – the other in the modern spirit.

But there is something still more striking in the evils which have resulted from the modern regardlessness of truth. Consider, for instance, its effect on what is called historical painting. What do you at present *mean* by historical painting? Now-a-days it means the endeavoring, by the power of imagination, to portray some historical event of past days. But in the Middle Ages, it meant representing the acts of *their own* days; and that is the only historical painting worth a straw. Of all the wastes of time and sense which Modernism has invented – and they are many – none are so ridiculous as this endeavor to represent past history. What do you suppose our descendants will care for our imaginations of the events of former days? Suppose the Greeks, instead of representing their own warriors as they fought at

Marathon, had left us nothing but their imaginations of Egyptian battles; and suppose the Italians, in like manner, instead of portraits of Can Grande and Dante, or of Leo the Tenth and Raphael, had left us nothing but imaginary portraits of Pericles and Miltiades? What fools we should have thought them! how bitterly we should have been provoked with their folly! And that is precisely what our descendants will feel towards us, so far as our grand historical and classical schools are concerned. What do we care, they will say, what those nineteenth century people fancied about Greek and Roman history! If they had left us a few plain and rational sculptures and pictures of their own battles, and their own men, in their every-day dress, we should have thanked them. "Well, but," you will say, "we *have* left them portraits of our great men, and paintings of our great battles." Yes, you have indeed, and that is the only historical painting that you either have, or can have; but you don't *call* that historical painting. You don't thank the men who do it; you look down upon them and dissuade them from it, and tell them they don't belong to the grand schools. And yet they are the only true historical painters, and the only men who will produce any effect on their own generation, or on any other. Wilkie was a historical painter, Chantrey a historical sculptor, because they painted, or carved, the veritable things and men they saw, not men and things as they believed they might have been, or should have been. But no one tells such men they are historical painters, and they are discontented with what they do; and poor Wilkie must needs travel to see the grand school, and imitate the grand school, an ruin himself. And you have had multitudes of other painters ruined, from the beginning, by that grand school. There was Etty, naturally as good a painter as ever lived, but no one told him what to paint, and he studied the antique, and the grand schools, and painted dances of nymphs in red and yellow shawls to the end of his days. Much good may they do you! He is gone to the grave, a lost mind. There was Flaxman, another naturally great man, with as true an eye for nature as Raphael, – he stumbles over the blocks of the antique statues – wanders in the dark valley of their ruins to the end of his days. He has left you a few outlines of muscular men straddling and frowning behind round shields. Much good may they do you! Another lost mind. And of those who are lost namelessly, who have not strength enough even to make themselves known, the poor pale students who lie buried forever in the abysses of the great schools, no account can be rendered; they are numberless.

And the wonderful thing is, that of all these men whom you now have come to call the great masters, there was *not one* who confessedly did not paint his own present world, plainly and truly. Homer sang of what he saw; Phidias carved what he saw; Raphael painted the men of his own time in their own caps and mantles; and every man who has arisen to eminence in modern times has done so altogether by his working in their way, and doing the things he saw. How did Reynolds rise? Not by painting Greek women, but by painting the glorious little living Ladies this, and Ladies that, of his own time. How did Hogarth rise? Not by painting Athenian follies, but London follies. Who are the men who have made an impression upon you yourselves – upon your own age? I suppose the most popular painter of the day is Landseer. Do you suppose he studied dogs and eagles out of the Elgin Marbles? And yet in the very face of these plain, incontrovertible, all-visible facts, we go on from year to year with the base system of Academy teaching, in spite of which every one of these men has risen: I say *in spite* of the entire method and aim of our art-teaching.

It destroys the greater number of its pupils altogether; it hinders and paralyzes the greatest. There is not a living painter whose eminence is not in spite of everything he has been taught from his youth upwards, and who, whatever his eminence may be, has not suffered much injury in the course of his victory. For observe: this love of what is called ideality or beauty in preference to truth, operates not only in making us choose the past rather than the present for our subjects, but it makes us falsify the present when we do take it for our subject. I said just now that portrait-painters were historical painters; – so they are; but not good ones, because not faithful ones. The beginning and end of modern portraiture is adulation. The painters cannot live but by flattery; we should desert them if they spoke honestly. And therefore we can have no good portraiture; for in the striving after that which is *not* in their model, they lose the inner and deeper nobleness which *is* in their model. I saw not long ago, for the first time, the portrait of a man whom I knew well – a young man, but a religious man – and one who had suffered much from sickness. The whole dignity of his features and person depended upon the expression of serene, yet solemn, purpose sustaining a feeble frame; and the painter, by way of flattering him, strengthened him, and made him athletic in body, gay in countenance, idle in gesture; and the whole power and being of the man himself were lost. And this is still more the case with our public portraits. You have a portrait, for instance, of the Duke of Wellington at the end of the North Bridge – one of the thousand equestrian statues of Modernism – studied from the show-riders of the amphitheater, with their horses on their hind-legs in the saw-dust.[5] Do you suppose that was the way the Duke sat when your destinies depended on him? when the foam hung from the lips of his tired horse, and its wet limbs were dashed with the bloody slime of the battle-field, and he himself sat anxious in his quietness, grieved in his fearlessness, as he watched, scythe-stroke by scythe-stroke, the gathering in of the harvest of death? You would have done something had you thus left his image in the enduring iron, but nothing now.

But the time has at last come for all this to be put an end to; and nothing can well be more extraordinary than the way in which the men have risen who are to do it. Pupils in the same schools, receiving precisely the same instruction which for so long a time has paralyzed every one of our painters, – these boys agree in disliking to copy the antique statues set before them. They copy them as they are bid, and they copy them better than any one else; they carry off prize after prize, and yet they hate their work. At last they are admitted to study from the life; they find the life very different from the antique, and say so. Their teachers tell them the antique is the best, and they mustn't copy the life. They agree among themselves that they like the life, and that copy it they will. They do copy it faithfully, and their masters forthwith declare them to be lost men. Their fellow-students hiss them whenever they enter the room. They can't help it; they join hands and tacitly resist both the hissing and the instruction. Accidentally, a few prints of the works of Giotto, a few casts from those of Ghiberti, fall into their hands, and they see in these something they never saw before – something intensely and everlastingly true. They examine farther into the matter; they discover for themselves the greater part of what I have laid before you to-night; they form themselves into a body, and enter upon that crusade which has hitherto been victorious. And which will be absolutely and triumphantly victorious. The great mistake which has hitherto prevented the public mind from fully going with them must soon be corrected. That mistake was the supposition that, instead of wishing to recur to the *principles* of the early ages, these men wished to bring back the *ignorance* of the early ages. This notion, grounded first on some hardness in their earlier works, which resulted – as it must always result – from the downright and earnest effort to paint nature as in a looking-glass, was fostered partly by the jealousy of their beaten competitors, and partly by the pure, perverse, and hopeless ignorance of the whole body of art-critics, so called, connected with the press. No notion was ever more baseless or more ridiculous. It was asserted that the Pre-Raphaelites did not draw well, in the face of the fact, that the principal member of their body, from the time he entered the schools of the Academy, had literally encumbered himself with the medals given as prizes for drawing. It was asserted that they did not draw in perspective, by men who themselves knew no more of perspective than they did of astrology; it was asserted that they sinned against the appearances of nature, by men who had never drawn so much as a leaf or a blossom from nature in their lives. And, lastly, when all these calumnies or absurdities would tell no more, and it began to be forced upon men's unwilling belief that the style of the Pre-Raphaelites *was* true and was according to nature, the last forgery invented respecting them is, that they copy photographs. You observe how completely this last piece of malice defeats all the rest. It admits they are true to nature, though only that it may deprive them of all merit in being so. But it may itself be at once refuted by the bold challenge to their opponents to produce a Pre-Raphaelite picture, or anything like one, by themselves copying a photograph.

Let me at once clear your minds from all these doubts, and at once contradict all these calumnies.

Pre-Raphaelitism has but one principle, that of absolute, uncompromising truth in all that it does, obtained by working everything, down to the most minute detail, from nature, and from nature only.[6] Every Pre-Raphaelite landscape background is painted to the last touch, in the open air, from the thing itself. Every Pre-Raphaelite figure, however studied in expression, is a true portrait of some living person. Every minute accessory is painted in the same manner. And one of the chief reasons for the violent opposition with which the school has been attacked by other artists, is the enormous cost of care and labor which such a system demands from those who adopt it, in contradistinction to the present slovenly and imperfect style.

This is the main Pre-Raphaelite principle. But the battle which its supporters have to fight is a hard one; and for that battle they have been fitted by a very peculiar character.

You perceive that the principal resistance they have to make is to that spurious beauty, whose attractiveness had tempted men to forget, or to despise, the more noble quality of sincerity: and in order at once to put them beyond the power of temptation from this beauty, they are, as a body, characterized by a total absence of sensibility to the ordinary and popular forms of artistic gracefulness; while, to all that still lower kind of prettiness, which regulates the disposition of our scenes upon the stage, and which appears in our lower art, as in our annuals, our commonplace portraits, and statuary, the Pre-Raphaelites are not only dead, but they regard it with a contempt and aversion approaching to disgust. This character is absolutely necessary to them in the present time; but it, of course, occasionally renders their work comparatively unpleasing. As the school becomes less aggressive, and more authoritative – which it will do – they will enlist into their ranks men who will work, mainly, upon their principles, and yet embrace more of those characters which are generally attractive, and this great ground of offense will be removed.

Again: you observe that as landscape painters, their principles must, in great part, confine them to mere foreground work; and singularly enough, that they may not be tempted away from this work, they have been born with comparatively little enjoyment of those evanescent effects and distant sublimities which nothing but the memory can arrest, and nothing but a daring conventionalism portray. But for this work they are not now needed. Turner, the first and greatest of the Pre-Raphaelites, has done it already; he, though his capacity embraced everything, and though he would sometimes, in his foregrounds, paint the spots upon a dead trout, and the dyes upon a butterfly's wing, yet for the most part delighted to begin at that very point where the other branches of Pre-Raphaelitism become powerless.

Lastly. The habit of constantly carrying everything up to the utmost point of completion deadens the Pre-Raphaelites in general to the merits of men who, with an equal love of truth up to a certain point, yet express themselves habitually with speed and power, rather than with finish, and give abstracts of truth rather than total truth. Probably to the end of time artists will more or less be divided into these classes, and it will be impossible to make men like Millais understand the merits of men like Tintoret; but this is the more to be regretted because the Pre-Raphaelites have enormous powers of imagination, as well as of realization, and do not yet themselves know of how much they would be capable, if they sometimes worked on a larger scale, and with a less laborious finish.

With all their faults, their pictures are, since Turner's death, the best – incomparably the best – on the walls of the Royal Academy; and such works as Mr. Hunt's "Claudio and Isabella" have never been rivaled, in some respects never approached, at any other period of art.

This I believe to be a most candid statement of all their faults and all their deficiencies; not such, you perceive, as are likely to arrest their progress. The "magna est veritas" was never more sure of accomplishment than by these men. Their adversaries have no chance with them. They will gradually unite their influence with whatever is true or powerful in the reactionary art of other countries; and on their works such a school will be founded as shall justify the third age of the world's civilization, and render it as great in creation as it has been in discovery.

And now let me remind you but of one thing more. As you examine into the career of historical painting, you will be more and more struck with the fact I have this evening stated to you, – that none was ever truly great but that which represented the living forms and daily deeds of the people among whom it arose; – that all precious historical work records, not the past, but the present. Remember, therefore, that it is not so much in *buying* pictures, as in *being* pictures, that you can encourage a noble school. The best patronage of art is not that which seeks for the pleasures of sentiment in a vague ideality, nor for beauty of form in a marble image; but that which educates your children into living heroes, and binds down the flights and the fondnesses of the heart into practical duty and faithful devotion.

FOOTNOTES

1. Liberate Rolls, preserved in the Tower of London, and quoted by Mr. Turner in his History of the Domestic Architecture of England.

2. This incident is not of Orcagna's invention, it is variously represented in much earlier art. There is a curious and graphic drawing of it, *circa* 1300, in the MS. Arundel 83, Brit. Mus., in which the three dead persons are walking, and are met by three queens, who severally utter the sentences,
"Ich am aferd."
"Lo, whet ich se?"
"Me thinketh hit beth develes thre."
To which the dead bodies answer –
"Ich wes wel fair."
"Such scheltou be."
"For Godes love, be wer by me."
It is curious, that though the dresses of the living persons, and the "I was well fair" of the first dead speaker, seem to mark them distinctly to be women, some longer legends below are headed "primus *rex* mortuus," etc.

3. Luke ii. 42, 49.

4. 1 Kings iii. 5.

5. I intended this last sentence of course to apply to the thousand statues, not definitely to the one in immediate question, which, though tainted with the modern affectation, and the nearest example of it to which I could refer an Edinburgh audience, is the work of a most promising sculptor; and was indeed so far executed on the principles asserted in the text, that the Duke gave Mr. Steele a sitting on horse-

back, in order that his mode of riding might be accurately represented. This, however, does not render the following remarks in the text nugatory, as it may easily be imagined that the action of the Duke, exhibiting his riding in his own grounds, would be different from his action, or inaction, when watching the course of a battle. I must also make a most definite exception in favor of Marochetti, who seems to me a thoroughly great sculptor; and whose statue of Cœur de Lion, though, according to the principle just stated, not to be considered a *historical* work, is an *ideal* work of the highest beauty and value. Its erection in front of Westminster Hall will tend more to educate the public eye and mind with respect to art, than anything we have done in London for centuries.

April 21st, 1854. – I stop the press in order to insert the following paragraph from to-day's *Times*: – "The Statue of Cœur De Lion. – *Yesterday morning a number of workmen were engaged in pulling down the cast which was placed in New Palace Yard of the colossal equestrian statue of Richard Cœur de Lion. Sir C. Barry was, we believe, opposed to the cast remaining there any longer, and to the putting up of the statue itself on the same site, because it did not harmonize with the building. During the day the horse and figure were removed, and before night the pedestal was demolished and taken away.*"

6. Or, where imagination is necessarily trusted to, by always endeavoring to conceive a fact as it really was likely to have happened, rather than as it most prettily *might* have happened. The various members of the school are not all equally severe in carrying out its principles, some of them trusting their memory or fancy very far; only all agreeing in the effort to make their memories so accurate as to seem like portraiture, and their fancy so probable as to seem like memory.

ADDENDA

I could not enter, in a popular lecture, upon one intricate and difficult question, closely connected with the subject of Pre-Raphaelitism – namely, the relation of invention to observation; and composition to imitation. It is still less a question to be discussed in the compass of a note; and I must defer all careful examination of it to a future opportunity. Nevertheless, it is impossible to leave altogether unanswered the first objection which is now most commonly made to the Pre-Raphaelite work, namely, that the principle of it seems adverse to all exertion of imaginative power. Indeed, such an objection sounds strangely on the lips of a public who have been in the habit of purchasing, for hundreds of pounds, small squares of Dutch canvas, containing only servile imitations of the coarsest nature. It is strange that an imitation of a cow's head by Paul Potter, or of an old woman's by Ostade, or of a scene of tavern debauchery by Teniers, should be purchased and proclaimed for high art, while the rendering of the most noble expressions of human feeling in Hunt's "Isabella," or of the loveliest English landscape, haunted by sorrow, in Millais' "Ophelia," should be declared "puerile." But, strange though the utterance of it be, there is some weight in the objection. It is true that so long as the Pre-Raphaelites only paint from nature, however carefully selected and grouped, their pictures can never have the characters of the highest class of compositions. But, on the other hand, the shallow and conventional arrangements commonly called "compositions" by the artists of the present day, are infinitely farther from great art than the most patient work of the Pre-Raphaelites. That work is, even in its humblest form, a secure foundation, capable of infinite superstructure; a reality of true value, as far as it reaches, while the common artistical effects and groupings are a vain effort at superstructure without foundation – utter negation and fallacy from beginning to end.

But more than this, the very faithfulness of the Pre-Raphaelites arises from the redundance of their imaginative power. Not only can all the members of the school compose a thousand times better than the men who pretend to look down upon them, but I question whether even the greatest men of old times possessed more exhaustless invention than either Millais or Rossetti; and it is partly the very ease with which they invent which leads them to despise invention. Men who have no imagination, but have learned merely to produce a spurious resemblance of its results by the recipes of composition, are apt to value themselves mightily on their concoctive science; but the man whose mind a thousand living imaginations haunt, every hour, is apt to care too little for them; and to long for the perfect truth which he finds is not to be come at so easily. And though I may perhaps hesitatingly admit that it is possible to love this truth of reality too intensely, yet I have no hesitation in declaring that there is *no hope* for those who despise it, and that the painter, whoever he be, who despises the pictures already produced by the Pre-Raphaelites, has himself no capacity of becoming a great painter of any kind. Paul Veronese and Tintoret themselves, without desiring to imitate the Pre-Raphaelite work, would have looked upon it with deep respect, as John Bellini looked on that of Albert Dürer; none but the ignorant could be unconscious of its truth, and none but the insincere regardless of it.

How far it is possible for men educated on the severest Pre-Raphaelite principles to advance from their present style into that of the great schools of composition, I do not care to inquire, for at this period such an advance is certainly not desirable. Of great compositions we have enough, and more than enough, and it would be well for the world if it were willing to take some care of those it has. Of pure and manly truth, of stern statement of the things done and seen around us daily, we have hitherto had nothing. And in art, as in all other things, besides the literature of which it speaks, that sentence of Carlyle is inevitably and irreversibly true: – "Day after day, looking at the high destinies which yet await literature, which literature will ere long address herself with more decisiveness than ever to fulfill, it grows clearer to us that the proper task of literature lies in the domain of Belief, within which, poetic fiction, as it is charitably named, will have to take a quite new figure, if allowed a settlement there. Whereby were it not reasonable to prophesy that this exceeding great multitude of novel writers and such like, must, in a new generation, gradually do one of two things, either retire into nurseries, and work for children, minors, and semifatuous persons of both sexes, or else, what were far better, sweep their novel fabric into the dust cart, and betake them, with such faculty as they have, *to understand and record what is true*, of which surely there is and forever will be a whole infinitude unknown to us, of infinite importance to us? Poetry will more and more come to be understood as nothing but higher knowledge, and the only genuine Romance for grown persons, Reality."

As I was copying this sentence, a pamphlet was put into my hand, written by a clergyman, denouncing "Woe, woe, woe! to exceedingly young men of stubborn instincts, calling themselves Pre-Raphaelites."[1]

I thank God that the Pre-Raphaelites *are* young, and that strength is still with them, and life, with all the war of it, still in front of them. Yet Everett Millais is this year of the exact age at which Raphael painted the "Disputa," his greatest work; Rossetti and Hunt are both of them older still – nor is there one member of the body so young as Giotto, when he was chosen from among the painters of Italy to decorate the Vatican. But Italy, in her great period, knew her great men, and did not "despise their youth." It is reserved for England to insult the strength of her noblest children – to wither their warm enthusiasm early into the bitterness of patient battle, and leave to those whom she should have cherished and aided, no hope but in resolution, no refuge but in disdain.

Indeed it is woful, when the young usurp the place, or despise the wisdom, of the aged; and among the many dark signs of these times, the disobedience and insolence of youth are among the darkest. But with whom is the fault? Youth never yet lost its modesty where age had not lost its honor; nor did childhood ever refuse its reverence, except where age had forgotten correction. The cry, "Go up, thou bald head," will never be heard in the land which remembers the precept, "See that ye despise not one of these little ones;" and although indeed youth *may* become despicable, when its eager hope is changed into presumption, and its progressive power into arrested pride, there is something more despicable still, in the old age which has learned neither judgment nor gentleness, which is weak without charity, and cold without discretion.

FOOTNOTES

1. Art, its Constitution and Capacities, etc. By the Rev. Edward Young, M.A. The phrase "exceedingly young men of stubborn instincts," being twice quoted (carefully excluding the context) from my pamphlet on Pre-Raphaelitism.

CRESCENT MOON PUBLISHING

web: www.crmoon.com e-mail: cresmopub@yahoo.co.uk

ARTS, PAINTING, SCULPTURE

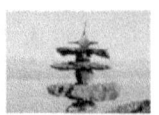
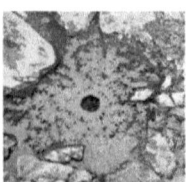
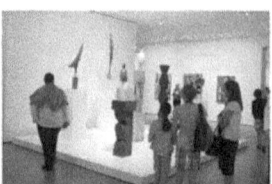
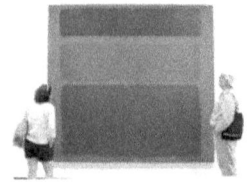

The Art of Andy Goldsworthy
Andy Goldsworthy: Touching Nature
Andy Goldsworthy in Close-Up
Andy Goldsworthy: Pocket Guide
Andy Goldsworthy In America
Land Art: A Complete Guide
The Art of Richard Long
Richard Long: Pocket Guide
Land Art In the UK
Land Art in Close-Up
Land Art In the U.S.A.
Land Art: Pocket Guide
Installation Art in Close-Up
Minimal Art and Artists In the 1960s and After
Colourfield Painting
Land Art DVD, TV documentary
Andy Goldsworthy DVD, TV documentary

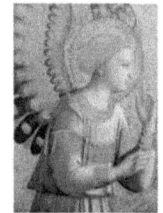

The Erotic Object: Sexuality in Sculpture From Prehistory to the Present Day
Sex in Art: Pornography and Pleasure in Painting and Sculpture
Postwar Art
Sacred Gardens: The Garden in Myth, Religion and Art
Glorification: Religious Abstraction in Renaissance and 20th Century Art
Early Netherlandish Painting
Leonardo da Vinci
Piero della Francesca
Giovanni Bellini
Fra Angelico: Art and Religion in the Renaissance
Mark Rothko: The Art of Transcendence
Frank Stella: American Abstract Artist

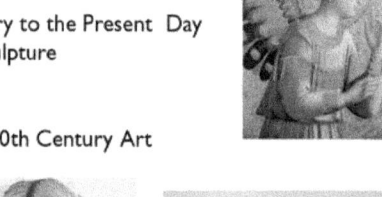
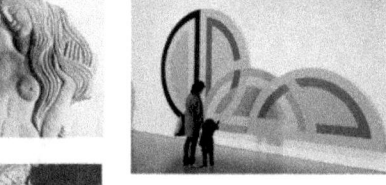

Jasper Johns
Brice Marden
Alison Wilding: The Embrace of Sculpture
Vincent van Gogh: Visionary Landscapes
Eric Gill: Nuptials of God
Constantin Brancusi: Sculpting the Essence of Things
Max Beckmann
Caravaggio
Gustave Moreau
Egon Schiele: Sex and Death In Purple Stockings
Delizioso Fotografico Fervore: Works In Process 1
Sacro Cuore: Works In Process 2
The Light Eternal: J.M.W. Turner
The Madonna Glorified: Karen Arthurs

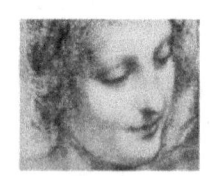
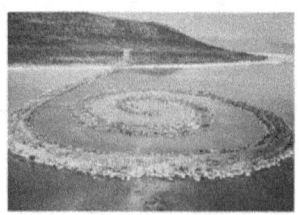

LITERATURE

J.R.R. Tolkien: The Books, The Films, The Whole Cultural Phenomenon
J.R.R. Tolkien: Pocket Guide
Tolkien's Heroic Quest
The *Earthsea* Books of Ursula Le Guin
Beauties, Beasts and Enchantment: Classic French Fairy Tales
German Popular Stories by the Brothers Grimm
Philip Pullman and *His Dark Materials*
Sexing Hardy: Thomas Hardy and Feminism
Thomas Hardy's *Tess of the d'Urbervilles*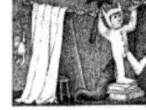
Thomas Hardy's *Jude the Obscure*
Thomas Hardy: The Tragic Novels
Love and Tragedy: Thomas Hardy
The Poetry of Landscape in Hardy
Wessex Revisited: Thomas Hardy and John Cowper Powys
Wolfgang Iser: Essays and Interviews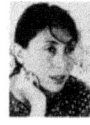
Petrarch, Dante and the Troubadours
Maurice Sendak and the Art of Children's Book Illustration
Andrea Dworkin
Cixous, Irigaray, Kristeva: The *Jouissance* of French Feminism
Julia Kristeva: Art, Love, Melancholy, Philosophy, Semiotics and Psychoanalysis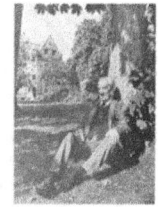
Hélene Cixous I Love You: The *Jouissance* of Writing
Luce Irigaray: Lips, Kissing, and the Politics of Sexual Difference
Peter Redgrove: Here Comes the Flood
Peter Redgrove: Sex-Magic-Poetry-Cornwall
Lawrence Durrell: Between Love and Death, East and West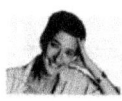
Love, Culture & Poetry: Lawrence Durrell
Cavafy: Anatomy of a Soul
German Romantic Poetry: Goethe, Novalis, Heine, Hölderlin
Feminism and Shakespeare
Shakespeare: Love, Poetry & Magic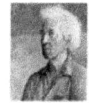
The Passion of D.H. Lawrence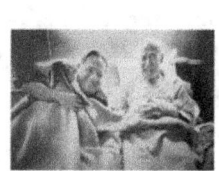
D.H. Lawrence: Symbolic Landscapes
D.H. Lawrence: Infinite Sensual Violence
Rimbaud: Arthur Rimbaud and the Magic of Poetry
The Ecstasies of John Cowper Powys
Sensualism and Mythology: The Wessex Novels of John Cowper Powys
Amorous Life: John Cowper Powys and the Manifestation of Affectivity (H.W. Fawkner)
Postmodern Powys: New Essays on John Cowper Powys (Joe Boulter)
Rethinking Powys: Critical Essays on John Cowper Powys
Paul Bowles & Bernardo Bertolucci
Rainer Maria Rilke
Joseph Conrad: *Heart of Darkness*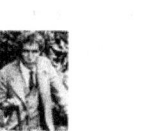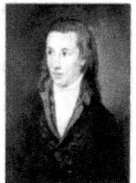
In the Dim Void: Samuel Beckett
Samuel Beckett Goes into the Silence
André Gide: Fiction and Fervour
Jackie Collins and the Blockbuster Novel
Blinded By Her Light: The Love-Poetry of Robert Graves
The Passion of Colours: Travels In Mediterranean Lands
Poetic Forms

POETRY

Ursula Le Guin: Walking In Cornwall
Peter Redgrove: Here Comes The Flood
Peter Redgrove: Sex-Magic-Poetry-Cornwall
Dante: Selections From the Vita Nuova
Petrarch, Dante and the Troubadours
William Shakespeare: Sonnets
William Shakespeare: Complete Poems
Blinded By Her Light: The Love-Poetry of Robert Graves
Emily Dickinson: Selected Poems
Emily Brontë: Poems
Thomas Hardy: Selected Poems
Percy Bysshe Shelley: Poems
John Keats: Selected Poems
Joh n Keats: Poems of 1820
D.H. Lawrence: Selected Poems
Edmund Spenser: Poems
Edmund Spenser: Amoretti
John Donne: Poems
Henry Vaughan: Poems
Sir Thomas Wyatt: Poems
Robert Herrick: Selected Poems
Rilke: Space, Essence and Angels in the Poetry of Rainer Maria Rilke
Rainer Maria Rilke: Selected Poems
Friedrich Hölderlin: Selected Poems
Arseny Tarkovsky: Selected Poems
Arthur Rimbaud: Selected Poems
Arthur Rimbaud: A Season in Hell
Arthur Rimbaud and the Magic of Poetry
Novalis: Hymns To the Night
German Romantic Poetry
Paul Verlaine: Selected Poems
Elizaethan Sonnet Cycles
D.J. Enright: By-Blows
Jeremy Reed: Brigitte's Blue Heart
Jeremy Reed: Claudia Schiffer's Red Shoes
Gorgeous Little Orpheus
Radiance: New Poems
Crescent Moon Book of Nature Poetry
Crescent Moon Book of Love Poetry
Crescent Moon Book of Mystical Poetry
Crescent Moon Book of Elizabethan Love Poetry
Crescent Moon Book of Metaphysical Poetry
Crescent Moon Book of Romantic Poetry
Pagan America: New American Poetry

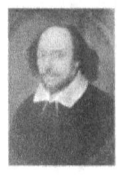
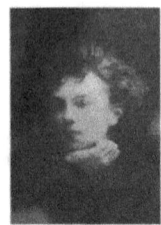
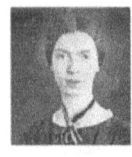
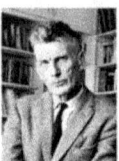
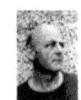
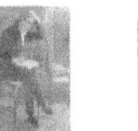
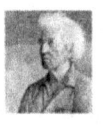
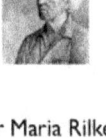
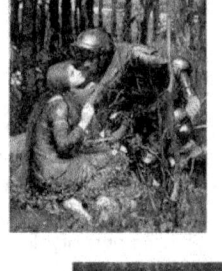
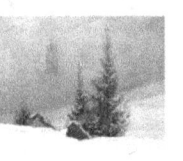
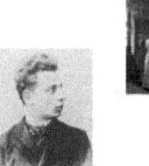
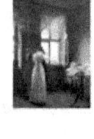
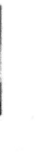
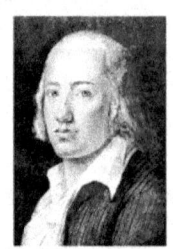

MEDIA, CINEMA, FEMINISM and CULTURAL STUDIES

J.R.R. Tolkien: The Books, The Films, The Whole Cultural Phenomenon
J.R.R. Tolkien: Pocket Guide
The *Lord of the Rings* Movies: Pocket Guide
The Cinema of Hayao Miyazaki
Hayao Miyazaki: *Princess Mononoke*: Pocket Movie Guide
Hayao Miyazaki: *Spirited Away*: Pocket Movie Guide
Tim Burton : Hallowe'en For Hollywood
Ken Russell
Ken Russell: *Tommy*: Pocket Movie Guide
The Ghost Dance: The Origins of Religion
The Peyote Cult
Cixous, Irigaray, Kristeva: The *Jouissance* of French Feminism
Julia Kristeva: Art, Love, Melancholy, Philosophy, Semiotics and Psychoanalysis
Luce Irigaray: Lips, Kissing, and the Politics of Sexual Difference
Hélène Cixous I Love You: The *Jouissance* of Writing
Andrea Dworkin
'Cosmo Woman': The World of Women's Magazines
Women in Pop Music
HomeGround: The Kate Bush Anthology
Discovering the Goddess (Geoffrey Ashe)
The Poetry of Cinema
The Sacred Cinema of Andrei Tarkovsky
Andrei Tarkovsky: Pocket Guide
Andrei Tarkovsky: *Mirror*: Pocket Movie Guide
Andrei Tarkovsky: *The Sacrifice*: Pocket Movie Guide
Walerian Borowczyk: Cinema of Erotic Dreams
Jean-Luc Godard: The Passion of Cinema
Jean-Luc Godard: *Hail Mary*: Pocket Movie Guide
Jean-Luc Godard: *Contempt*: Pocket Movie Guide
Jean-Luc Godard: *Pierrot le Fou*: Pocket Movie Guide
John Hughes and Eighties Cinema
Ferris Bueller's Day Off: Pocket Movie Guide
Jean-Luc Godard: Pocket Guide
The Cinema of Richard Linklater
Liv Tyler: Star In Ascendance
Blade Runner and the Films of Philip K. Dick
Paul Bowles and Bernardo Bertolucci
Media Hell: Radio, TV and the Press
An Open Letter to the BBC
Detonation Britain: Nuclear War in the UK
Feminism and Shakespeare
Wild Zones: Pornography, Art and Feminism
Sex in Art: Pornography and Pleasure in Painting and Sculpture
Sexing Hardy: Thomas Hardy and Feminism

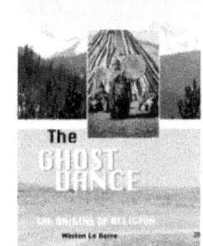
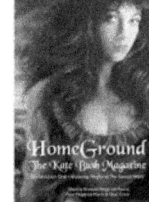
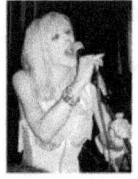
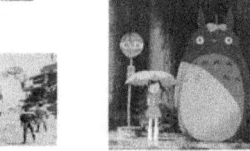
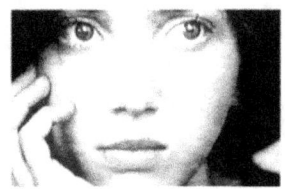

The Light Eternal is a model monograph, an exemplary job. The subject matter of the book is beautifully organised and dead on beam. (Lawrence Durrell)
It is amazing for me to see my work treated with such passion and respect. (Andrea Dworkin)

CRESCENT MOON PUBLISHING
P.O. Box 1312, Maidstone, Kent, ME14 5XU, Great Britain. www.crmoon.com

cresmopub@yahoo.co.uk   www.crescentmoon.org.uk